D. H. LAWRENCE

An Unprofessional Study

D. H. LAWRENCE

An Unprofessional Study

by Anais Nin

with an Introduction by

Harry T. Moore

THE SWALLOW PRESS INC.

CHICAGO

Fourth Printing

Published by
The Swallow Press Incorporated
1139 South Wabash Avenue
Chicago, Illinois 60605

This book is printed on 100% recycled paper.

ISBN 0-8040-0067-0
LIBRARY OF CONGRESS CATALOG NUMBER 64-16109

Contents

*"...The critic's task is to compare a work
with its own concrete standard of truth..."*
                              Henry James

Introduction

by HARRY T. MOORE

When D. H. Lawrence had been dead for two years, in 1932, a young girl in Paris published a book about him. The girl was Anaïs Nin, and the book is the present one, which has long deserved reprinting.

Miss Nin's career since 1932 may be briefly summarized. She has written a number of remarkable novels and volumes of stories which have won her a special public. Her books include *Children of the Albatross, House of Incest, Under a Glass Bell, This Hunger, The Four-Chambered Heart, A Spy in the House of Love, Seduction of the Minotaur,* and *Winter of Artifice.* Fortunately these volumes are available in editions issued by Alan Swallow, the Denver publisher who has for so many years sponsored some of the finest writing of our time. Miss Nin's books have received tributes from critics of the stature of Edmund Wilson and Rebecca West, who like so many other readers have been engaged by the sensitivity and sensibility of this writing which goes beneath the surface realism of our day to the astounding reality beneath.

Besides her fiction, Miss Nin has devoted much of her time to a project that will probably prove to be one of the most exciting literary achievements of our century. This is her famous diary, only small parts of which have been published — enough to indicate its importance as a document and as a work of literature. Miss Nin began it during a time of perplexity and stress in childhood, and she has faithfully kept it going until it has now supposedly reached hundreds of volumes. These will one day see the light, though perhaps not until the mechanics of reproduction and publication have advanced enough

7

to put such voluminous work easily within range of most readers; those of us who will miss this can only envy them.

To get back to D. H. Lawrence: something should be said about the situation in 1932. Because of the present huge fame of Lawrence it is hard for those of us who can not remember how he was regarded in his lifetime, and just after his death, to realize how much he was unappreciated and how often he was sneered at. He had a small and faithful public, a few thousand readers who provided him royalties enough to live on just above the line of poverty. But with few exceptions, the reviewers of his works were either condescending or savage, and the wide public knew of Lawrence only as a man whose books were sometimes suppressed. His death in 1930 brought forth some bitter obituaries, still shocking as one looks over them today. A few friends of Lawrence defended him — Richard Aldington, Catherine Carswell, Lady Ottoline Morrell, and John Middleton Murry — against the general nastiness of the press. A most generous word came from E. M. Forster, who knew Lawrence slightly; in contradiction to the belief that prevailed in Bloomsbury, Forster spoke of him as the greatest imaginative novelist of his generation. And the tone of this statement contrasted with such slanderous accounts of Lawrence as the obituary notice of him in the *New Yorker* by Genêt (Janet Flanner), who during the second world war was to defend Pétain! Genêt in her "report" said that Lawrence felt that his "writer friends," as well as Dr. Carl Jung, had stolen his ideas. Now I have written a critical biography of Lawrence and a straight biography, both built on a great deal of source material, and I have edited his *Collected Letters* in two volumes running to more than 1200 pages; and I can say clearly that among this material I have found no evidence whatever to support this ridiculous accusation of Genêt's. Nor is there any truth in her sensational picture of Lawrence as having, "among other eccentricities, a fancy for removing his clothes and climbing mulberry trees."

8

This is the kind of trash that prevailed in supposedly responsible publications. And it kept up for years. That is why Miss Nin's book was so refreshing in 1932: it saw Lawrence as a writer, a great writer, and it sensitively explored his work.

There had been some other books about Lawrence, including a good one in 1930 by Stephen Potter, *D. H. Lawrence: A First Study*. But in 1931, Murry's *Son of Woman* severely damaged Lawrence's reputation. Murry, as noted earlier, had been one of those to defend Lawrence from the vicious death notices; but as he began to brood over his relationship with Lawrence, Murry came up with a strange book. He wanted, wanted very hard, to praise his friend and at least parts of his writing, but his own tormented relationship with Lawrence became entangled in the story. Suffice to say that Murry was usually a good critic — of people he didn't know.

Two books by women, besides Miss Nin's, came out in the following year. Mabel Dodge Luhan's *Lorenzo in Taos* was enough to arouse disquiet about Lawrence if only because readers might wonder why a first-rate writer could put up with anyone so utterly off balance as Mrs. Luhan, in her own words, showed herself to be. But authors are not always fortunate in those who surround them; the Taos experience evokes memory of Matthew Arnold's comment on the Shelley circle: "What a set! what a world!" Lawrence, however, still had his defenders, with Catherine Carswell's *The Savage Pilgrimage* in 1932 (attacked the following year in Middleton Murry's *Reminiscences of D. H. Lawrence*), and with another friendly volume, the Hon. Dorothy Brett's *Lawrence and Brett: A Friendship*, in 1933. But enough books have been mentioned to provide the setting for a brief discussion of Anaïs Nin's. It came out at a time when Lawrence wasn't being examined critically but biographically: the great question in literary circles then was not whether *Women in Love* was a great novel, but whether Lawrence had thrown crockery at his wife Frieda. True, in 1933, Horace Gregory brought out a fine critique, *Pilgrim of the Apocalypse* — a volume which underestimated *Women in Love* but is still a valuable study.

The Nin and Gregory volumes, however, were not enough to distract the attention of the public from the warring biographies. Lawrence disappeared during the depression and the second world war because readers considered him irrelevant; they failed to see that Lawrence had been the prophet of just such catastrophies, failed to see what a somewhat changed Murry pointed out in 1956, not long before his own death — that "Lawrence was alone in the depth of his prescience of the crisis of humanity which has developed since his death." Indeed, it was not until the 1950s, with the appearance of such fine interpretations as Father Martin Jarret-Kerr's *D. H. Lawrence and Human Existence* (1951, revised 1961), that Lawrence came critically into his own. There have been several other excellent interpretations of Lawrence, and now we have this welcome reprint of Miss Nin's pioneering work, modestly subtitled *An Unprofessional Study.*

My own copy is dated "Paris 1932" on the flyleaf, and contains a statement by its Paris publisher, Edward W. Titus, to the effect that he had printed five hundred and fifty copies of the book, "numbered 1 to 500 for subscribers, and fifty copies, numbered 501 to 550 for the press. This is No. 323." That my admiration for this book lasted is shown by what I said of it in 1951, in the first edition of my own volume, *The Life and Works of D. H. Lawrence,* which states that Miss Nin's study "is one of the most valuable books on Lawrence because of its discussion of the *texture* of his work." At this moment, a new version of *The Life and Works* is being printed in New York, and although I haven't a copy of the text at hand, I certainly didn't change that statement.

Note the reference to Miss Nin's discussions of the *texture* of Lawrence's work. Consider these statements from her book:

Lawrence's language makes a physical impression because he

projected his physical response into the thing he observed. . . . His sensorial penetration is complete. That is why his abstract thought is always deep reaching: it is really concrete, it passes through the channels of the senses. . . . Lawrence attempted some very difficult things with writing. For him it was an instrument of unlimited possibilities; he would give it the *bulginess of sculpture,* the feeling of heavy material fulness: thus the loins of the men and women, the hips and the buttocks. He would give it the nuances of paint: thus the efforts to convey shades of color with words that had never been used for color. He would give it the rhythm of movement, of dancing: thus his wayward, formless, floating, word-shattering descriptions. He would give it sound, musicality, cadence: thus words sometimes used less for their sense than their sound. It was a daring thing to do. Sometimes he failed. But it was certainly the crevice in the wall, and opened a new world to us.

It would be hard to come closer than this to Lawrence's magic. The quotation above is compressed from several passages that should be read in their fullness, as the reader of this book will be able to do. I want to make it clear at once that Anaïs Nin's study doesn't deal only with Lawrence's texture, but also with the force of his expressional power. It is of course difficult if not impossible to detach these elements from the ideas to which they give flesh; Miss Nin doesn't make the mistake of trying to do so. Her fine understanding of what Lawrence was trying to do in such books as *The Rainbow, Women in Love, Kangaroo,* and *Lady Chatterley's Lover* enriches the understanding of us all in relation to those novels. She knew what Lawrence was about:

Lawrence concentrated on the pursuit of an experience with all the slow, intricate, laborious elements of his own nature. He grew within the novel, in a devious way which is the despair of the formalists. What he discovered in the multitudinous byways of his fancies and his intuitions was sometimes unessential, sometimes unique.

11

The particular kind of intuition — emotional knowledge — for which we are so grateful in Miss Nin's own later fiction, she first applied to her explication of Lawrence. Surely this book was an important stage in her own development. In that diary she had kept from girlhood, she had become a seasoned observer of life, a seasoned writer; but in making her first public appearance in print with this sensitive interpretation of Lawrence, she probably stepped across the distance from girlhood into young womanhood. And what she so wonderfully knew in youth, and could see in Lawrence's writings, is still very valuable, valuable to all of us. How good it is to have this book born again.

Southern Illinois University
November 28, 1963

The Approach
to D. H. Lawrence's World

"The business of the mind is first and foremost the pure joy of knowing and comprehending, the pure joy of consciousness."

The world D. H. Lawrence created cannot be entered through the exercise of one faculty alone: there must be a threefold desire of intellect, of imagination, and of physical feeling, because he erected his world on a fusion of concepts, on a philosophy that was against division, on a plea for whole vision: "to see with the soul and the body." For the world he takes us into is shadowed, intricate. It is "ultimately chaos, lit up by visions, or not lit up by visions."

It is therefore above all the world of the poets and it is the preponderance of the poet in him that is the key to his work. He magnified and deepened experience in the manner of a poet.

The most characteristic attitude of the true Lawrence is a state of high seriousness and lyrical intensity.

His philosophy was not a coolly constructed formula, an assemblage of theories fitting reasonably together: it was a *transcending of ordinary values,* which were to be vivified and fecundated by instincts and intuitions. To such intuitional reasoning he submitted himself and all his characters.

Thus to begin to realize Lawrence is to begin immediately to realize philosophy not merely as an intellectual edifice but as a passionate blood-experience.

13

He had both a tender and a violent, a sober and an extreme way of probing feelings and entanglements. Beneath the pounding and the sharpness we must sense the poet who works through visions and the primal consciousness. "The primal consciousness in man is pre-mental and has nothing to do with cognition."

Reading Lawrence should be a pursuit of his intuitions to the limit of their possibilities, a penetration of his world through which we are to make a prodigious voyage. It is going to be a prodigious voyage because he surrenders fully to experience, lets it flow through him, and because he had that quality of genius which sucks out of ordinary experience essences strange or unknown to men.

Lawrence has no system, unless his constant shifting of values can be called a system: a *system of mobility*. To him any stability is merely an obstacle to creative livingness.

"Commandments should fade as flowers do. They are no more divine than flowers are... There is a principle of evil. The principle of resistance to the life principle.

"If a man loves life, and feels the sacredness and mystery of life, then he knows that life is full of strange and subtle and even *conflicting imperatives*. And a wise man learns to recognize the imperatives as they arise — or nearly so — and to obey. But most men bruise themselves to death trying to fight and overcome their own, new, life-born needs, life's ever strange imperatives. The secret of all life is obedience: obedience to the urge that arises in the soul, the urge that is life itself, urging us to new gestures, new embraces, new emotions, new combinations, new creations."

Lawrence's World

In the beginning, the idyllic beginning, when difficulties are felt only through a half-dim consciousness, Lawrence has ample freedom to observe the background, and we have the classical, almost naïve surface landscape painting of the *White Peacock*.

As Lawrence the poet evolves, the background becomes ominous, as in *Sons and Lovers*. Further on it becomes symbolical, as in *Twilight in Italy*. There, while descriptions of nature are richer than ever, it is their reflection in the mind and feelings which becomes more essential. As he discovers the universe and pierces the crust of the earth with his personal vision, the background becomes more and more symbolical.

And now begins in Lawrence that consciousness of planes: of twofold and multiple planes.

There is the plane of the visible universe, nature, houses, churches, collieries, movies — the artist's eye sees them all; there is the plane of corresponding thought perpetually at work at its task of understanding and transforming. This is all an upper plane, in the head, the brain. Then there is the plane of subconscious life in continuous flow and movement, with its own wisdom and its own impulses: the solar plexus, the blood-consciousness. (Blake's *Marriage of Heaven and Hell*.) "The blood consciousness is the first and last knowledge of the living soul: the depths."

15

"...The absolute need which one has for some sort of satisfactory mental attitude toward oneself and things in general makes one try to abstract some definite conclusions from one's experiences as a writer and as a man. The novels and poems are *pure passionate experiences.* These" (the two books on Psychology) "are made afterwards, from the experiences."

So we shall first study the experiences.

Since his world is the enlargement of his own gigantic imagination, out to· see and to experience all, the characters have their roots in reality, but they are soon dissociated from familiar moulds and absorbed by Lawrence. He is at work on such a vast, almost impersonal comprehension, that realities are not sufficient: he must use symbols.

Probabilities of the literal kind do not bother him, and his dialogue is as often impossible as possible, his situations unreal as real. He is outside of that. A great part of his writing might be called "interlinear" because of his constant effort to make conscious and articulate the silent subconscious communications between human beings.

First of all he asks us to begin at the beginning of the world with him. By his own questions, put as seriously as a child's, and with a child's obstinacy, he will take each man back to the beginning of the world, as if each had to settle it all for himself, begin his own world, find his god. *(The Boy in the Bush.)*

To retrogress with Lawrence is to question every value, and thus begins his reversal of ordinary values.

It is an effort to recapture genuine evaluations, like those of children before they are taught. A child will say to an older person who has been playing with him and participating wholeheartedly in his make-believe: Are you older than me? How can that be?

How can that be if the older person has been playing, conceiving fancies with him? The child does not see any difference, if age is a closeness to death, and death is simply not being able to play, not being alive in feeling. The child is looking *at the essence quality of livingness,* not at any outward appearance of age, which is irrelevant.

Thus Lawrence says with the same pure, profound disregard of appearances: everything is either alive or dead, according to transcendental definitions of life and death.

Lawrence's chief preoccupation is precisely the choice between life and death, or rather: between *complete life and death. Livingness* is the axis of his world, the light, the gravitation, and electromagnetism of his world.

Experiences

Lawrence approaches his characters not in a state of intellectual lucidity but in one of *intuitional reasoning*. His observation is not *through the eyes but through the central physical vision* — or instinct. His analysis is not one of the mind alone, but of the senses.

In his characters there is usually a double current of life: there is the act of living with corresponding articulateness, and there is also the *articulateness of dreams*, in symbols.

He recognized a deep, subterranean connection between what he called the "dark gods" in us, entirely apart from the sophistries of the intelligence. Lawrence had divined that the intelligence is a juggler, an adroit juggler who can make everything balance and fall right. But the "'dark gods" are instinctive, undeceived, undeceivable. They are intent on that flow of blood-life. We have tried to deceive them in our modern life. We have felt mind, the juggler, omnipotent. Lawrence is hostile to the juggler.

> "And don't, with the nasty, prying mind, drag it"
>   (sex) "out from its deeps
> and finger it and force it, and shatter the rhythm it keeps
> when it's left alone, as it stirs and rouses and sleeps."

(The deeps are also the "darkness." There is "beauty and dignity in the darkness.")

When the realization came to the moderns of the importance of vitality and warmth, they willed the warmth with their minds. But Lawrence, with the terrible flair of the genius, sensed that a mere mental conjuring of the elemental was a perversion.

So here are his people struggling to achieve *complete life* and a sincere understanding of the gods in the *center of our bodies*.

Lawrence believed that the feelings of the body, from its most extreme impulses to its smallest gesture, are the warm root for true vision, and from that warm root can we truly grow. The livingness of the body was natural; the interference of the mind had created divisions, the consciousness of wrong-doing or well-doing.

Imprisoned in our flesh lives the body's own genie, which Lawrence set out to liberate. He found that the body had its own dreams, and that by listening attentively to these dreams, by surrendering to them, the genie can be evoked and made apparent and potent.

He well knew that often the body's dreams came out in awkward or ugly forms. Many modern realistic novels showed to what triteness these dreams had dwindled — pitiful, graceless attempts.

Lawrence was patient. He gave his characters time. (*The Lost Girl*.) They are to find their own way and hour of resurrection. It was very slow, this gaining of confidence in the wisdom of the body. So Lawrence was patient, through a maze of timidities, retractions, blunders, awkwardnesses.

In *Sun* a woman gives herself to the sun, and is "vivified." Her body now *walks* beautifully, and her soul is realized. The life-flow stirred in her is a state of grace. The object to which her realization now urges the woman is unimportant. With the creator's strange indifference to personalities, Lawrence pursues a more important creation. It does not matter that the woman in *Sun* now desires a peasant. It matters that the woman now *desires*. Lawrence raises us to a plane of vital, impersonal creation and recreation.

19

Why should not an impulse be wise, or wisdom become impulsive?

"Real knowledge comes out of the whole corpus..."

Life is a process of *becoming*, a combination of states we have to go through. Where people fail is that they wish to elect a state and remain in it. This is a kind of death.

Did Lawrence remain in this state of physical consciousness, in the mere efflorescence of his blood-life? No. We shall see later how he progressed from this point in his own way.

Meanwhile he did want to bring us into the plenitude of this physical state so that from there we could go along with him. But at the very first step of his philosophy he encountered opposition. *The Rainbow* was burned by the authorities.

In himself he was utterly convinced of the soundness of his philosophy. No man ever wavered less in his convictions. But he was waiting for the world to catch up with him and so he remained long on this first ground, propounding, pleading, emphasizing and re-emphasizing his ideas. This accounts for much in his work that seems redundant and over-emphatic.

But there was another reason.

Lawrence had been educated a Christian, the neutral, inoffensive (to society), restrained kind. He, himself, has found it very difficult to express his "primordial flow." In the world about him the mind and the will were supreme, and it required something like a miracle to reestablish confidence in the wisdom of the flesh.

His accents, while those of a man who knew how deeply right he was, exposed the relentless struggle within himself to throw off the mind and the will he was born with and to let the miracle accomplish itself in him.

In *Kangaroo*, where Lawrence himself is most revealed, there are curious pages.

Somers (Lawrence) and Harriet see Jack and Victoria, the next-door neighbors, openly express their feelings for each other.

"Victoria looked up with a brightly-flushed face, entirely unashamed, her eyes glowing like an animal's. Jack relaxed his grip on her but did not rise" (to accompany the Somers who are leaving).

And the Somers leave precipitately, and with distaste. " 'Well,' said Harriet, 'I think they might have waited just two minutes before they started their love making. After all, one doesn't want to be implicated, does one?' "

And Somers agrees.

This is a most un-pagan reaction. It is a revelation of hypersensitiveness and self-consciousness which is in clear contradiction with Lawrence's philosophy. But it is true to his feelings.

There is another moment when Somers realizes that Victoria is silently offering herself to him. But he refuses.

"Why not follow the flame, the moment sacred to Bacchus? Why not if it was the way of life? He did not know why not. Perhaps only old moral habit. It was Victoria's high moment —; all her high moments would have this Bacchic weapon-like momentaneity: Should not a man know the whole range? *But his heart of hearts was subbornly puritanical.*"

When William Blake was constructing his world he made no attempt to exteriorize his imaginings in his own life; he knew that the time had not come. His life would have been a failure, and unconvincing. His poetry and prose had been flung out beyond his own boundaries, to *future generations*. He was content to live as others did, to go on perfecting his prophecies and his visions.

The very nature of Lawrence's philosophy, on the other hand, forbade any attempt on his part at detachment. His convictions were the emanations of a *life deeply lived* through all its failures and contradictions. He was personally involved. And this personal presence that we feel in Lawrence's world gives it a warmth lacking in other prophets. He gave much

21

of his strength; and over and over again he exposed himself recklessly to bitter criticism and hostility because he would not evade the last test of his sincerity. He gave of his own blood. The denial and detachment of Blake is a sacrifice. But so is the giving of blood.

Lawrence had that quality of genius which makes a man realize experiences unknown to other men.

Middleton Murry tells us in his *Reminiscences of D. H. Lawrence* that Lawrence wanted "men who would understand a bit along with him... it was beyond the experience of his friends to go along with him." Murry admits that "somewhere in ourselves we were set against the experiences he wanted us to partake... there were realms of experiences, which Lawrence knew, which I had not entered. Even now I cannot pretend that the fearful struggle between Anna Lensky and Will Brangwen in *The Rainbow* is a thing I understand."

Had Lawrence detached himself so much from current human problems that he could not be understood by the intelligent men of his time? Precisely that. He detached himself from the current human problems which current writers could fathom.

There was an unknown world within the known. He had a vision. Will it take us one hundred years to understand Lawrence's vision as it took us one hundred years to understand Blake's?

What were those experiences his friends could not enter with him?

Anna Lensky and Will Brangwen marry. They spend their honeymoon alone in a cottage, absorbed in each other. It is all blissful, and soothing, and complete. He discovers all kinds of little traits in her that he likes; she in him. Her blitheness is a balm to him. He feels that he is born anew.

"He surveyed the rind of the world: houses, factories, trams, the discarded rind; people scurrying about, work going on, all on the discarded surface. An earthquake (the marriage) had

22

burst it all from the inside. It was as if the surface of the world had been broken away entirely: Ilkeston, streets, church people, work, rule-of-the-day, all intact; and yet peeled away into unreality, leaving here exposed the inside, the reality: one's own being, strange feelings and passions and yearnings and beliefs and aspirations, suddenly become present, revealed to the permanent bedrock, knitted one rock with the woman one loved."

Thus he is dreaming. But Anna is suddenly roused to activity and wants to give a tea party.

"The wonder was going to pass away again. All the love, the magnificent new order was going to be lost, she would forfeit it all for the *outside things*. She would admit the outside world again, she would throw away the living fruit for the ostensible rind. *He began to hate this in her.*"

It is not the tea party: Will could not hate her because she wants to give a tea party. But in the light of deeper values, the tea party is a disaster. It reveals to Will that Anna loves the *outside* things. Now this is important. It indicates a whole difference between them. He senses the portentousness of it, senses the division which will take place later. To a mere tea party the reaction is excessive. As a symbol, it is comprehensible. Women have always done their reasoning and drawn inferences from such *trifles*. It has been termed pettiness. Women are intuitive: the trifle is an ominous sign, a direct warning of a greater issue ahead. It is the betraying ripple on the surface. Man's logic is against *a priori* deductions from isolated trifles. But that is the way women "reason" and Lawrence employs the same method.

Now Will is deeply disappointed, and Anna does not understand why.

"His soul grew blacker" and he is hard, recoiled. Now she is hurt in her own sensitiveness, and infers the existence in him of a darkness, recoil, and hardness, which frighten her.

Finally when she cries they kiss and are reconciled, but the struggle has been violent, not in proportion to the event, but in proportion to that conflict beginning in them.

They go to church together.

In church he "wanted a dark, nameless emotion, the emotion of all the great myteries of passion... She could not get out of church the satisfaction that he did... Her mind is set against mystic experience." So she is exasperated because he has a power to escape from her into ecstasy. She moves about, drops her glove, knocks him, to annoy and arouse him. And she does not know why she is angry.

Later he is looking over illuminated books of symbolical images. She jeers at his absorption.

"He was partly ashamed of the ecstasy into which he could throw himself with these symbols..." But her laughter and indifference to them is agony to him. He hates her again. He leaves her alone. But when he comes back, black and surly, his anger has abated. "She had broken a little of something in him."

Physical love unites them again.

We are far from the tea party, but the tea party was the beginning of the same conflict. And now it is set deeper.

They are enemies, as many men and women in love with each other are enemies. Making use of their love, the blood-connection, to assert their will over each other, or to alter each other's inner world.

"They fought an unknown battle, unconsciously. Still they were in love with each other..." Because their love is in danger of death, the struggle is fierce in them.

"She wanted to be happy, to be natural, like the sunlight and the busy daytime... And he wanted her to be dark, unnatural."

"Dark" and "unnatural" are Anna's way of describing the thoughtfulness, the deep feelings of her husband.

"She had thought him just the bright reflex of herself."

There is much cruelty, and moments of partial understanding.

"Then he loved her for her childishness and for her strangeness to him, for the wonder of her soul which was different from his soul..."

Only a moment. "She begins to combat his deepest feelings." She scoffs at miracles, and he "tastes of death... Because his life was formed in these unquestioned precepts."

They irritate, torture each other.

When she begins to bear him children, she is Anna Victrix. He cannot combat her anymore. And she lapses into vague content.

"She was not with him... A pang of insufficiency would go over him as he heard her talking to the baby... He stood near, listening, and his heart surged, surged to rise and submit. *Then it shrank back and stayed aloof.* He could not move, a denial was upon him, as if he could not deny himself. He must, *he must be himself*."

The struggle never ends. The humanness in Anna is also a glowing thing, which attracts him. He wishes he could understand, or at least be wholly satisfied.

All this is easily translated as the projection of the little things of life into their larger significance, as we begin to see below the surface and become altogether conscious.

But there remains unexplained the intensity of Lawrence's description of these experiences. They are important, profound, but must the style be so tense, the expressions so extreme? Do people really swing from one extreme emotion to another in so short a span? We know that poets do.

Lawrence is giving his characters an extreme sensibility, the power of the poets; see how they can fall into mystic trances in church, can flare into demoniac anger, brood, or pass rapidly from despair to bliss. "—Life always a dream, or a frenzy," to the poet.

Lawrence often probes so intensely the significance of persons or events that they are sometimes deformed out of their normal shapes and become abstractions. But this habit of deformation of the normal is merely poetic means to an end, an end which is understanding. Through the intensity of his emotion for the smaller he divines the meaning of the greater. This is a justification for what at first glance may seem exaggerated or even obsessional.

For the same reason Lawrence does not create what we generally understand by a "character," that is, a definitely outlined being who bears a resemblance to those we know. He does not give such a clear outline because the personages in his books are symbolical; he is more preoccupied with the states of consciousness and with subconscious acts, moods, and reactions. His characters act by deeper and more chaotic motives than those in ordinary novels: they are experiments — subjected to all the shiftings of experimental living. They are more sensitive to the laws of subconscious actions than to the formulas by which ordinary people live down their subconscious. And as Lawrence's delving is new, in the sense that delving into chaos is a characteristic of our epoch, and none other, he himself was aware of the imperfections and difficulties, and that is why he afterwards elucidated and analyzed his ideas in books of essays and psychology.

The key to his characters, then, or the simplest way of understanding them, is to think of them as artists. There is another example of this in *The Rainbow*. In this book the violent union of Anton and Ursula is devastating, and at first sight, incomprehensible. They seek violently in each other a satisfaction they do not find. Yet the experience is not a purely animal one — its meaning is not confined to a sexual struggle — it expresses at the same time another struggle, another craving. It is no mere sexual phenomenon, but more truly *the creator's craving for a climax far bigger than the climaxes life has to offer*. It is symbolical of the creative voraciousness which is, as a general instinct, unsatisfiable, because it is out of proportion with the universe, with the realities surrounding him. It is the allegory of the urge which was never meant to be answered but merely to exist, like the urge to live in spite of, and even because of the certain knowledge of death, to live in the largest possible "circuitous way towards death," in Freud's words.

Now when the creator submits to that urge for livingness it almost destroys him because his emotional receptivity is in proportion to the extreme of his desire and his hunger. That Lawrence did not mean this as a merely sexual struggle is clear for another reason (Lawrence never means what is literally apparent). It symbolizes also the search for balance in physical love. Lawrence realized the tragedy of inequality in love as no one else ever realized it. And with it he realized the tragedy not alone of physical but of spiritual and mental love which is the cause of torment in human relationships. It is inequality of sexual power which causes disintegration in sexual relationships. Each man and each woman must find his own level. If Lawrence had not meant that, the union of Lady Chatterley and Mellors would not have been a fulfilment, while that of Anton and Ursula proved destructive. It was a fulfilment because the former were balanced forces, while Anton and Ursula were not. Ursula was too strong for Anton.

It is this struggle for balance which is at the basis of Lawrence's descriptions of love and hate, destruction and creation, between men and women. He was aware of the see-saw rhythm in relationships.

Rebecca West has given us a beautiful interpretation of Lawrence's intensity in her 'Elegy": "When he cried out at Douglas for shaking hands with the innkeeper because the North and the South were enemies, and when he saw the old crones who had come to cheat him out of an odd lira or two over the honey as Mænads too venomous even to be flamboyant, I thought he was seeing lurid colours that were in his eyes and

27

not in the universe he looked on. Now I think *he was doing justice to the seriousness of life, and had been rewarded with a deeper insight into its nature than most of us have.*"

* * *

The intensity of *The Nightmare* in *Kangaroo* is easier to understand just because Lawrence has called it a nightmare. He has in a way drawn a boundary line. We are entering a nightmare, but it is *reality,* heightened by a terrific effort at comprehension. It is the story of the individual's fearful struggle to remain sane in spite of the madness of the mob when it accepts war.

The whole meaning of the war for Lawrence is in the Nightmare. "It was the whole spirit of the war, the vast mob-spirit which he could never acquiesce in. The terrible, terrible war, made so fearful because in every country practically every man lost his head, and lost his own centrality, his own manly isolation in his own integrity, which alone keeps life real.

"Plenty of superb courage to face death. But no courage in any man to face his isolated soul and abide by its decisions. Easier to sacrifice one's self."

Because many, many men thought and felt as Lawrence did. But many preferred death to isolation. Many preferred death rather than denying a dead ideal — for war was one of the dead ideals.

"It is not death that matters, but the loss of the integral soul." And: "*I won't have popular lies.*" That is Lawrence's frequent cry: "I won't have popular lies." But popular lies are immense, and powerful, and they would have none of Lawrence.

And there is a moving example here of Lawrence's peculiar loyalty to his own body: Somers has been found unfit, as Lawrence had been. "Somers did not care. 'Let them label me unfit,' he said to himself. 'I know my own body is fragile, in its way, but also it is very strong, and it's the *only body that would carry my own particular self.'* " Surely individuality was never so absolute in any man.

Somers "had nothing to do but hang on to his own soul. So he hung on to it, and tried to keep his wits... the plank was his own individual soul."

But why should this attitude be accompanied by such intensity of feeling? The egoist holds on emotionessly to his own plank. The fundamental reason for Lawrence's emotional condition is that he is sensitive, fearfully and profoundly so: he suffers, he suffers much from pity, tenderness, horror — he participates with feeling. What drives him to despair is his very conviction of the sacredness of the body — and war is a monstrous holocaust of innumerable bodies.

There is always in Lawrence on the one hand the individualist struggling for isolation, on the other the man tormented with pity, with his feeling of kinship, with a desire for understanding with his fellow-men. And this tenderness it is, as well as the rejection of his tenderness, which makes him violent. Fighting the world he fights his own tenderness. That is the reason for his intensity. Mere egoists are not intense in this way. Their withdrawal is self-preservation. Fruit sweetened, preserved, in complacent peace.

And as for the *Englishness* of Lawrence it is in Somers: "One of the most intensely English little men England ever produced, with a passion for his country, even if it were often a passion of hatred."

*　*　*

If the reality of the war is compared to a nightmare, dreams are often realities. To the poet the experience of a dream is no different from the experience of reality. "Life always a dream or a frenzy." There is no boundary line. Through other books Lawrence had dreamed, and had fancies, had improvised, and people could only say: *This* is chaos, *this* is nonsense.

The boundary line exists only for those who always want to return to the first peace and security. They carefully mark the way of their wandering for recognition on the way back: *This* is a dream, *this* is a fantasy; I only have to deny that they have any connection with myself, only to say that they are accidents, fragments, fluid, for them to diappear like ghosts. And I will be with my real self again.

But in Lawrence's books dreams and reality are often interwoven just as they are in our own natures.

In *St. Mawr*, in *The Rainbow*, in *Women in Love* the boundaries are undetectable. Where the allegory begins, where the symbolism, where the images, where the drama, it is impossible to say.

In *The Rainbow* Ursula goes for a walk on a stormy afternoon. She has just resolved that "'woman was a giver of life,'" and that she would return to her husband, and bear him children, and give up all the intricate desires and aspirations of her secret inner world.

The rain and storm are a "fluctuation." After a long while she wants to "beat her way back through all this fluctuation, back to stability and security." The instability is not in the storm, but in her own mental conflict, and she is going back to a decision, to shelter.

"Suddenly... some horses were looming in the rain, not near yet. *But they were going to be near.* She continued her path inevitably. There were horses in the lee of a clump of trees beyond, above her. She pursued her way with bent head. *She did not want to lift her face to them.* She did not want to know they were there. She went on in the wild track. *She knew the heaviness on her heart.* It was the weight of the horses. But she would circumvent them. She would bear the weight steadily, and so escape... Suddenly the weight deepened and her heart grew tense to bear it. *Her breathing was laboured.* But this weight also she could bear... She was aware of the great flash of hoofs... the horses thundered upon her...." She is broken

30

by the struggle to escape. She lies faint and still on the roadside.

Ursula's decision to return to Skrebensky, to bear his children, has extended into the whole world. The world, woods, and storm are to become *images* of the feelings which torment her. Nature is to re-enact her fluctuations and her fears. The horses are symbols of maternity and the sexual experience of marriage. Now the whole page reads differently: "There were horses in the lee of a clump of trees beyond, above her... *She did not want to lift her face to see them.*"

She did not want to face the full consequences of her decision.

But: "she knew the heaviness of her heart."

Her heart is over-full of aspirations, dreams, and desires for another kind of life.

"It was the weight of the horses."

It was the weight of maternity and purely physical existence.

"But she would bear the weight steadily and so escape."

Perhaps through living as a wife and mother, through denial, she can still preserve her inner life intact.

"Her breathing was laboured."

As it would be in child-bearing.

"The great flash of hoofs" is the sexual pounding in her womb.

* * *

Such entanglements in relations between men and women, between reality and unreality, fantasies and life, are denied by most people.

The first analysis of an event or a person yields a certain aspect. If we look at it again, it has another face. *The further we progress in our reinterpretation, the more prismatic are the moods and the imaginings coordinating the facts differently each time.* People who want a sane, static, measurable world take the first aspect of an event or person and stick to it, with an almost self-protective obstinacy, or by a natural limitation of their imaginations. They do not indulge in either deepening or magnifying.

But others know that the imagination is a constant deformer. It needs to be, it must be, in order to be capable of extending from comparatively small happenings, in a comparatively short span of life. Otherwise to understand one thought, on feeling, we would have to go through a thousand experiences. But one experience can be multiplied by our imagination. And it is this power to multiply and to expand which creates at the same time intricacies and entanglements. Entanglements are the other face of the same activity.

In the conflict of Anna and Will, the death of Gerald, the nightmare, and the horse fantasy, we are given the clues to more than one kind of conflict, one kind of obsession, one kind of nightmare. And this is simply the *fundamental basis of poetic creation* with which Lawrence has animated his characters.

The love and hate alternating in men and women, as in *Women in Love* is due to the same profound sense of oscillation, of flux and reflux (Herakleitos), revulsions and convulsions, *mobility. The becoming always seething and fluctuating.*

There can never be, according to Lawrence, a perfect relationship between people. We are doomed to solitariness.

"This individuality which each one of us has got and which makes him a wayward, wilful, dangerous, untrustworthy quantity to every other individual, because every individuality is bound to react at some time against every other individuality, without exception — or else lose its own integrity; because of the inevitable necessity of each individual to react away from any other individual, at certain times, human love is truly a relative thing, not an *absolute*."

Lawrence's descriptions of the undercurrents of body and mind were but means of bringing to the surface many feelings that we do not sincerely acknowledge in ourselves. Freud and Jung have also done this, but they are essentially scientists and they are read with the detachment and objectivity of scientific research. Lawrence's characters, whether in poetry, allegory, or prophecy, are actors who speak with the very accents of our emotions; and, before we are aware, our feelings become identified and involved with theirs. Some have recoiled from such an awakening, often unpleasant; many have dreaded having to acknowledge this power of their physical sensations, as well as to face in plain words, the real meaning of their fantasies.

Lawrence was reviled for going so far. *There are always those who fear for that integral kernel in themselves, for that divine integrity which can be preserved by ignorance* (before psychology) *or by religion* (before and after psychology) *or by the cessation of thought* (by the modern paroxysm of activity).

So it was not the truth, but the stirring, live quality in Lawrence's truth which upset people. Besides the scientists there were novelists like André Gide and Aldous Huxley who had left nothing unexplored. But Huxley and Gide traveled with the intellect and with that upper strata in the head, and therefore as they went along we were *hit in our heads,* and the experience took on a scientific aspect, became pure abstract knowledge.

Huxley was his Philip: "*...loyal only to the cool indifferent flux of intellectual curiosity.*" There is nothing more devastating to ordinary standards of value than pages of Gide's *L'Immoraliste* and pages of Huxley's *Point Counterpoint.*

But Lawrence went at the reversal of values not with indifference but with poetry, with religious fervor, and he *hit lower* than either Huxley or Gide. He hit the center, the vulnerable center of our bodies with his *physical language,* his *physical vision.* He hit us vitally.

And the self-protective, integrity-preserving instincts of society rose bitterly against him.

Lawrence had been unforgivably persuasive.

He had not only thought about everything but he had felt

everything, and he greatly cared, and so we were forced to care, and his voice had strange, potent accents.

And as no one would go along with him, he went alone, through hell. And the more experiences he went through, the more he understood. The more you know about hell, the more you know about heaven. The more you know of decadence, the more virile the reaction back to livingness.

* * *

Love between men. His mind deliberated here, long enough to give more qualms to his self-preserving friends.

More oscillations.

There was an equation in the love between men and women. Was it the only creative one? Lawrence doubted pat equations. There was a suspicious dignity, decorum, and facility about them. Truth had a more vagabond air, and dwelt in chaos and oscillation. Perhaps oscillation was the right permanent state of being, and perhaps a creative and natural one too.

The assumption of what is natural may rise out of a wrong premise. Many errors had slipped down unnoticed through the centuries. The family was a unit which was eminently useful to society. Society had a genius for making everything that was useful appear to issue from religious decrees, divine dictates. Society was very intelligent in the care of itself. The family taught kindness, self-sacrifice, and fecundity. Fecundity was useful in war time.

Love between men and women might not be the only basis of life. The fact that they were biological complements did not mean that they were always mental complements.

So Lawrence speculates on the value of the association of man with man. Wherever there is an under-current attachment and flow, there is life. Here he seeks more keenly than ever the truth concealed under appearances. The apparent physical completeness of the love of man and woman may not be the only completeness. Everything was possible in a state of livingness which transcends human laws, or in a nature which contradicts itself and is constantly feeling its way, blunderingly, contradictorily. There was the possibility that feelings might run in two streams.

If you go very far all values shift. It will not do to stay on the same ground forever. If you are terribly truthful, the ground will always move from under you, and you will have to shift with the constantly shifting truth. (System of mobility.)

After all, if we let the whole universe flow through us, then our experiences become fluid, run into new shapes.

There are things Lawrence likes to do, and to talk over with men, and it is with men that a man works at the building of his world. There is an association and a community of interest.

In *Kangaroo*, Somers: "...loved working with John Thomas ... picking, or resting, talking in the intervals with John Thomas, who loved a half-philosophical, mystical talking about the sun, and the moon, the mysterious powers of the moon at night, and the mysterious change in man with the change of season, and the mysterious effects of sex on a man...

"Poor Harriet spent many lonely days in the cottage. Somers was not interested in her now... Then would come. John Thomas with the wain, and the two men would linger putting up the sheaves, lingering, talking, till the dark, talking of the half-mystical things with which they were both filled."

The same is true with Gerald and Birkin in *Women in Love*.

But it is in *Aaron's Rod* that Lawrence went through hell. Here the matter of connection and flow between men reaches a peak of anxiety. There is a desire for connection, but how is it to be answered?

The fact that he concludes that between men there must be a relationship not based on sex is important — "He dreamed a new human relationship. A stark, stripped human relationship of two men, deeper than the deeps of sex. Deeper than property, deeper than fatherhood, deeper than marriage, deeper than love. So deep that it is loveless. The stark, loveless, wordless unison of two men who have come to the bottom of themselves." But even more important is that he *understood* — understood the subterranean flowing together of men as part of a state of being.

With this understanding he will continue the creation of his world — a more complete world because of the understanding. A world closed to no true state of body or soul.

He is "liberated from the laws of idealism." Of ordinary idealism. Ordinary idealism is composed mainly of dead ideals.

"But evening is also the time for revelry, for drink, for passion. Alcohol enters the blood and acts as the sun's rays. It inflames into life, it liberates into energy and consciousness. But by a process of combustion. That life of the day which we *have not lived*, by means of sun-born alcohol we can now flare into sensation, consciousness, energy and passion, and live it out. It is a liberation from the laws of idealism, a release from the restrictions of control and fear. It is the blood bursting into consciousness. But naturally the course of the liberated consciousness may be in either direction: sharper mental action, greater fervor of spiritual emotion, or deeper sensuality."

Alcohol and sun are symbols. Fearless experience, passionate experience accomplish the same thing. Lawrence's world is liberated not from idealism but from dead ideals. He is constantly making lists of dead ideals (as the ideal of war in *Kangaroo*). For ideals also have a fundamental mobility: they are born and they die. And to stick to dead ideals is to die.

Lawrence had completed his cycle. There has been a progression, but not a strictly philosophic progression since Lawrence has stated the whole of his philosophy before in other books. Philosophically, then, *Lady Chatterley's Lover* is not a climax.

He has said this before: "When a man and woman truly come together, when there is a marriage, then an unconscious

36

vital connection is established between them like a throbbing blood-circuit. A man may forget a woman entirely with his head, and fling himself with energy and fervor into whatever job he is tackling, and all is well... if he does not break that inner vital connection which is the mystery of marriage... *The most immediate union is woman, the wife."*

What then has been the real climax of progression in Lawsence? There has been a *progression in perfection,* and the climax is in the *perfection.* (It is unnecessary to dwell on the occasional retrogression — the imperfections and technical weaknesses, since they are quite unimportant in an ultimate valuation of his work.)

Lady Chatterley's Lover is, as we shall see, a more perfect expression of his mystical attitude towards the flesh than any other book he wrote.

But: "...does all life work up to the one consummating act of coition? In one direction it does... But we are not confined to one direction only, or to one exclusive consummation. Was the building of cathedrals a working up towards the act of coition? Was the dynamic impulse sexual? No... there was something else, of even higher importance and greater dynamic power.

"And what is this other greater impulse? It is the desire of the human male to build a world, to build a world out of his own self and his very own belief and his own effort, something wonderful. Not merely useful. Something wonderful."

So Mellors, Lady Chatterley's lover, at the end of the book, turns to the building of a world.

The Religious Man

Lawrence was in reality a profoundly religious man, in his search for God which he pursued all through his life, and in his personal conception of God. For in spite of his non-conformity he realized God.

In his *Assorted Articles* he confesses that the banal hymns of his childhood had penetrated through him even more deeply than the loveliest poems.

"No geographical knowledge ever divested the Lake of Galilee of its wonder."

And what is wonder? "It is the natural religious sense."

The hymns were never "subjected to an critical analysis," and they retained their wonder.

But under critical observation other dogmas disappeared. "One can save one's pennies. How can one save one's soul? One can only *live* one's soul. The business is to live, really live. And this needs wonder."

And so Lawrence lived with wonder. Whatever was beatifically congealed, static, was dead.

And here comes again Lawrence's acknowledgement of *"instinctive wisdom"*: "...when I was about seven, a woman teacher was trying to harrow us about the Crucifixion. And she kept saying: 'And aren't you sorry for Jesus? Aren't you sorry?' And most of the children wept. I believe I shed a crocodile tear or two, but very vivid is my memory of saying to myself.: 'I don't really care a bit.' And I could never go back on it. I never cared about the Crucifixion, one way or another. Yet the *wonder* of it penetrated very deep in me."

And what is wonder? "A natural religious sense."

So Lawrence was naturally religious, true to his deep instinctive sense of religion.

Having this natural-wonder religious sense at the *core* he is not afraid to speculate on the essence of Christ. And as it is always the *livingness* which is the essence, he wonders how it is that the church is always loudly asserting: " 'We preach Christ crucified.' In so doing, they preach only half of the Passion, and do only half their duty. The Creed says: Was crucified, died and was buried... the third day He rose again from the dead. And again: I believe in the resurrection of the body... So that to preach Christ Crucified is to preach only half the truth."

So here is Lawrence himself at his work of resurrection, the work he loves.

He is to resurrect Christ too.

"Christ-child, in the lap of the woman, and again, Christ crucified: then the Mass, the mystery of atonement through sacrifice. Yet all this is really preparatory, these are the preparatory stages of the real living religion... Yet a vast mass of Christians stick there."

Why?

"Because great religious images are only images of *our own experiences,* or of our own state of mind and soul."

So man's experience was: "himself as Christ-child, standing on the lap of a Virgin Mother."

"During the war, this image broke in the hearts of most men... During the war the man who suffered most bitterly suffered beyond the help of wife or mother, and no wife, nor mother, nor sister, nor any beloved, could save him from the guns. The fact went home in his heart, and broke the image of mother and Christ-child and left in its place the image of Christ crucified... *consummatum est!* It is finished."

But the young who never went through the war "cannot accept the Christ crucified finality... they came into life and found everything finished... Now man cannot live without some vision of himself. But still less can he live with a vision that is not true to his inner experience and inner feeling. For even after Atonement men still must live, and must go forward with the vision."

And so: "Christ risen in the flesh!" is revealed to Lawrence, or rather, Lawrence, because of his instinct for resurrection, discovers the resurrection of Christ.

"Christ risen in the full flesh!"

And Lawrence, with his usual open, shadowless, infinite sincerity, looks at the Church with these words on his lips, and finds that the Church holds back, that people hold back. People are again afraid.

Lawrence is again judged. He is left alone.

His usual fearlessness of mind and soul is blasphemous. Profaning what? Half-truths in twilit souls — profaning the neutrality and the peace.

So Lawrence goes alone again, to the end of his experience.

"And Jesus was risen flesh and blood. He rose a man on earth to live on earth. The greatest test was still before Him: His life as a man on earth...

"This is the image of our inward state today: the teaching is over, the sacrifice is made, the salvation is accomplished. Now comes the true life, man living his full life on earth, as flowers live their full life, without rhyme or reason, except the magnificence of coming forth into fulness.

"He rose to become at one with life, to live the great life of the flesh and the soul together — to take a woman to Himself... to know the tenderness and blossoming of the twoness with her..."

Lawrence is gone again on a solitary journey. We hang back — perhaps for a hundred years.

* * *

In *The Boy in the Bush* there is a quest for God. The boy

is looking for a Father. He is not looking for any beatific, voiceless void, or idol, gold-dusted and unapproachable.

"The God he called on was a dark, almost fearful mystery... Yourself is God. It wasn't true. There was a terrible God somewhere else... inside of himself he was alone... Somewhere *outside* himself was a terrible God who decreed..."

But a little later Jack feels differently. He has been fighting venomous people, he has tamed animals, he has used his sixth sense in the forest; Monica has stirred him; he has known solitude. So he says: "After all, perhaps the very best thing was to be alone. Because where you are alone you are at *one* with your own God. *The spirit in you is God in you.* And when you are alone you are one with the spirit of God inside you."

Easu is the Antichrist. The boy Jack loathes him, and wants to go on loathing him. He wants even to kill him, with the consent of his God — with whom he now holds very "chummy" talks. And when the moment comes, his God consents. *His* God, of course, *not* the God of his aunts and his pastor.

Here too Lawrence reveals, and not for the first time, his conviction of God in *man* — in man, not in woman. Monica the woman, must give herself up to Jack. "He demanded this submission as if it were a submission to his mysterious Lord." (They are both now so identical with each other!) "She would never submit to the mysterious Lord direct." (She did not *realize* God.) "And yet yield before the immense Lord she must. Through him."

Of course, if the building of the world, creation, was entrusted to man, and he had his way of communing with the Lord — the woman must commune with the Lord through man. Why it should be thus arranged is difficult for the modern woman to understand. The modern woman desires also to build her own world directly, not through the man. But Lawrence would have it so for the *woman*. The woman who creates a world directly (art or business) is the artist-builder woman. She is not provided for in Lawrence's metaphysics. But the *core* of her is. He was thinking of Woman the emanation, the complement, "woman who was only a part thing by herself, a fragment..."

Part of Lawrence's religion is sun-worship. He has many an incantation to the sun. Here he simply takes note of it on his way to a kind of religion: "...the immense assertive vigour and sacred handsomeness of the sun... the wild, immense, fierce, untamed sun, fiercer than a glowing-eyed lion with a vast mane of fire, crouching on the western horizon, staring at the earth as if to pounce on it, the mouse-like earth.

"And there is another glory of the moon... the immense liquid gleam following... with a great miraculous liquid smile." Both of these now become symbols to him — like night and day in *Twilight in Italy* — two different powers — two aspects of his own being.

"And when the flame came up in him, tearing from his bowels, in the sudden new desire for Monica, this was his spiritual body, the body transfigured with fire."

Whatever way he turns he must make sex mystical, part of his religion, a fundamental part of it. His religion is to have roots, marvelous, *warm roots*.

Neither Mary nor Monica are entirely satisfactory, and this arouses in Jack a tormenting duality. They are not right in relation to his religion. Monica is at variance with God because she thinks He will not let her be natural, and she wants to be natural. Mary's God is the God of man's roughly made laws. So when Jack tells Mary he wants both her and Monica — "At the present moment I'm not Monica's... the sun goes, and the moon comes. A man isn't made up of one thread" — Mary clings to formulas: "but you *should* love Monica only," and sets herself against the wisdom of her own body, which urges her to yield.

"She was a piece of the upholstered world."

He cannot have his Old Testament "many wives," but he refuses to be tamed.

"Everybody... wants to destroy me... even passively... because inside of my soul I don't conform; can't conform. They would all like to kill the non-conforming me. Which is myself!"

The eternal struggle of the individual against society.

Jack will not submit to society. He is defeated in the creation of his material world, but not in the creation of himself. In that he is superb, arrogant, even hopeful.

It is not Jack who "rode over the crest and down the silent grey bush, in which he had once been lost." It is Lawrence. He rides alone, but with his God.

* * *

Lawrence's travels are often pilgrimages.

In Italy he makes a long, strange, insistent way of the Cross, with ample meditations. *(Twilight in Italy.)*

In *Kangaroo* his religion is also expressed in the words of the leader: "The salvation of souls seems too speculative a job. I think if a man is truly a man, true to his being, his soul saves itself in that way. But no two people can save their souls alive in the same way. As far as possible, we must leave it to them."

The conception of the multiplicity of God, that is, many gods in every man, and the conception of individual gods as individual possessions is also more explicitly stated in *Kangaroo*:

"And into every living soul wells up the darkness, the unutterable. And then there is the travail of the visible with the invisible. Man is in travail with his own soul, while ever his soul lives. Into his unconscious surges a new flood of the God-darkness, the living unutterable. And this unutterable is like a germ, a fœtus with which he must travail, bringing it at last into utterance, into action, into *being*.

43

"The long travail. The long question of the soul within a man and the final parturition, the birth of a new way of knowing, a new God-influx... This time not a God scribbling on tablets of stone or bronze. No everlasting decalogues. No sermons on mounts, either. The dark God, forever unrevealed. The God who is *many gods to many men*: all things to all men. The source of passion and strange motives..."

Death

Since Lawrence's philosophy was so fundamentally based on a conception of "livingness" it is not surprising that his first emotional reaction towards the idea of death was one of utter horror and protest.

In *The Boy in the Bush*: "Death, the great end and goal. Death the black, void, pulsating reality which would swallow them all up like a black lover finally possessing them. The great black fleshliness of the end, the huge body of death reeling to swallow them all. And for this they danced, and for this they loved and reared families and made farms: to provide good meat and white, pure bones for the black, avid horror of death."

In *Women in Love* Gerald watches his father die with "a great red-hot stroke of horrified fear."

"It was a trial by ordeal. Could he stand and see his father slowly dissolve and disappear in death, without once yielding his will, without once relenting before the omnipotence of death... The real activity was this ghastly wrestling for death in his own soul. And his own will should triumph. Come what might he would not bow down or submit or acknowledge a master. He had no master in death... the fearful space of death..."

Gerald cannot struggle alone. His instinct leads him to the woman — to balance. He seeks to loose the "pent-up darkness and corrosive death" in the miracle of physical renewal.

That is all, for Gerald. Love against death — the unbearable idea of death.

When Ursula reaches a moment of despair she contemplates death in another way. Emptiness in life is more unbearable than death. In other words, death in life is more terrible than physical death. And it is the death in life that Lawrence never knew.

"But physical death is a consummating experience. It is a development from life. One must go where the unfaltering spirit goes, there must be no balking the issue, because of fear." In all this there is a defeat, because Ursula feels death as a void, or a sleep. But as she thinks about it more, Lawrence reveals his own second mood and *triumph over death*:

"And she knew, with the clarity of ultimate knowledge that the body is only one of the *manifestations of the spirit, the transmutation of the integral spirit is the transmutation of the physical body as well.*

"To die is to move on with the invisible. To die is also a joy, a joy of submitting to that which is greater than the known, namely, the pure unknown. That is a joy... There is no ignominy in death. Life indeed may be ignominious, shameful to the soul. But death is never a shame."

The Return to the Primitive

It is in the handling of this problem that Lawrence has proved again his great *sanity*.

Every period in history has culminated in a return to primitive nature, but each return has usually ended with more regard for forms than for any real assimilation of the primitive qualities. Rousseau popularized shepherd costumes and farm houses, as if for a masquerade or carnival.

"Here at last is Rousseau's Child of Nature, and Chateaubriand's Noble Savage called upon and found at home."

It was said that Lawrence advocated such a primitive life for ourselves. "He had lived among the Indians, you know."

In *Classical Studies in American Literature* he gives a summary of his own conclusions: "The truth of the matter is *one cannot go back*. Some men can: renegades... I could never go back. Back towards the past, savage life. One cannot go back. It is one's destiny inside one.

"There are these people, these 'savages.' One cannot, does not despise them. One does not feel superior. But there is a gulf, in time and being. I cannot commingle my being with theirs."

What he admired in the Indian dances which he described with such vividness, was the "wholeness" of the Indian, his concentration, his unity of being. There are not in him any divisions created by separate consciousness. That was wonderful to Lawrence, tired of the effort at coordination we make with our separate faculties.

But there is need of a *renewal*. "What are they doing? Who knows? But perhaps they are giving themselves to the pulsing incalculable fall of the blood, which forever seeks to fall to the center of the earth, while the heart, like a planet pulsating in an orbit, keeps up the strange, lonely circulating of the separate human existence."

Again the idea of renewal takes the form of a burrowing into the earth, to the *sources of life*. We find this same feeling in his description of the "night-consummation" in *Fantasia of the Unconscious*: "As the night falls and the consciousness sinks deeper, suddenly the blood is heard hoarsely calling. Suddenly the deep centers of the sexual consciousness rouse to their spontaneous activity. Suddenly there is a deep circuit established betwen me and the woman. Suddenly the sea of blood which is me heaves and rushes towards the sea of blood which is her. There is a moment of pure frictional crisis and contact of blood. And then all the blood in me ebbs back into its ways, transmuted, changed. And in this renewal lies the great magic of sex. For it is a liberation, a perfected sex-circuit."

But we cannot stay at the source all the time.

With his usual truthfulness Lawrence, while admiring the Indian dances, asserts that there can never be any close association with or communing with the primitives.

"'We can't go back. We can take a great curve in their direction, onward... Yet as I say, we must make a *great swerve* in our onward-going life-course now, to gather up again the savage mysteries. But this does not mean going back on ourselves."

Woman

Lawrence was chided for his antediluvian ideas on woman. They were not antediluvian, but again to be translated in terms of quintessences. His intuitive intelligence sought the *core* of the woman. *The core of the woman is her relation to man.*

The woman for whom the phallic worship is only half of creative divinity is the builder-artist. Lawrence was not meddling with that builder-artist direction taken by women, but with the woman within the builder-artist. Woman pure and simple — or neither pure nor simple.

Taken as such, what was an adequate or inadequate woman?

In *The Jeune Fille Wants to Know* he reflects merrily on the outspokenness of the modern jeune fille and one feels that he delights in it.

He makes a humorous portrait of Laura Philipine: " 'What are boys for 'xcept to jazz with,' she says. 'But what about when you're thirty and forty?' 'Oh, I suppose they'll invent new dances all the time.' "

In *Give Her a Pattern* he understands the problem of woman, who has effaced her real self in order to satisfy man-made images. Men had the images, they conceived the patterns — women carried them out to please the men. Dante made the Beatrices, and Dickens the child-wife, and the modern young man the little-boy-baby-face girl.

"But women are not fools... they have their own logic. A woman may spend years living up to a masculine pattern. But in the end the strange and terrible logic of emotion will work

49

out the smashing of the pattern, if it has not been emotionally satisfactory."

Of course, the woman-artist, who was herself an image maker, a pattern maker, made her own images and her own patterns. Georges Sand was Georges Sand all through. In fact, a revelation to men. So was Madame de Staël — absolute self-created individualities. So were Jane Austen and George Eliot, Amy Lowell, and so, today, is Ruth Draper.

Now the proportion of artist-builder women has increased, and with it women's power to create their own images and their own patterns, in all professions, occupations and arts, for their own profound satisfaction. And here comes Lawrence to admit that most men's patterns *had not been much good.* "What could a woman possibly give to a man who wanted a baby-boy face? What could she possibly give him but the dribblings of an idiot?"

I would call this an extremely sympathetic feeling for the problems of the modern woman!

Then Lawrence analyzes the *instinctive knowledge* of woman in an ironic allegory.

"There are two aspects to women. There is the demure and the dauntless."

But "we don't expect a girl skilfully driving a car to be demure, we expect her to be dauntless."

However: "The girl who has got to make her way in life has got to be dauntless, and if she has a pretty, demure manner with it, then lucky girl. She kills two birds with two stones."

Why? "Because demureness is outwardly becoming..."

One gathers from this that Lawrence is giving delicate hints to the artist-builder in outward becomingness.

"There are also two kinds of confidences: there are the women who are cocksure and the women who are hensure. A really up-to-date one is a cocksure woman. She doesn't have a doubt or a qualm. She is the modern type. Whereas the old-fashioned demure woman was sure as a hen is sure, that is, without knowing anything about it. She went quietly and busily clucking around, laying the eggs and mothering the chickens in a kind of anxious dream that still was full of sureness. Her sureness was a physical condition..."

Now the cock: "crows because he is *certain* it is day. Then the hen peeps out from under her wing. He marches to the door of the hen-house and pokes out his head assertively. '*Ah, ha! daylight of course, just as I said!*...' The hen accepts it entirely... From the house a person ought to appear scattering corn. Why does the person not appear? The cock will see to it. He is cocksure. He gives a loud crow in the doorway, and the person appears. The *hens are suitably impressed*.... So the day goes on.

"But in her own dim surety, the hen is really much surer than the cock in a different way. She marches off to lay her egg, she secures obstinately the nest she wants, she lays her egg at last, then steps forth again with prancing confidence, and gives that most assured of all sounds, the hensure cackle of a bird who has laid an egg..."

The modern woman, however, "has stepped forth and called the sun out of bed." But having also the hensurenes besides, she is too sure also of the importance of calling the sun out of bed. She *overdoes* it. And besides: "they find often, that instead of having laid an egg, they have laid a vote, or an empty ink-bottle, or some other absolutely *unhatchable* object, which means nothing to them."

Lawrence is quite conscious of the tragedy of this situation. The woman does not want to live in dim sureness, with purely domestic, material proofs of her activity: eggs — but neither is the man's life a satisfaction to her. Lawrence does not say anything against her except that cocksureness does not suit her. He implies that she might have done a great deal with her hensureness — her own instinctive wisdom. Let the cock call the sun out of bed with his own magnificence — if she be feminine in her ways, — and to be feminine is to be like the hen, suitably impressed by the effectiveness of the cock's crowing — if she be feminine when the moment comes, he will also be magnificent with her. And she will have both the vote and the hatchable egg.

* * *

Relations between men and women. Lawrence has already said several times that there cannot be a perfect relationship, that is, one without conflict. And this is his clearest explanation:

"The individuality which each of us has got and which makes him a wayward, wilful, dangerous, untrustworthy quantity to every other individual, because every individuality is bound to react at some time or other against every other individuality without exception — or else lost its own *integrity;* because of the inevitable necessity of each individual to react away from any other individual, at certain times, *human love is truly a relative thing, not an absolute. It cannot be an absolute.*"

But there again we have clung desperately to an idea of absolute, and this is the real cause of the tragedy: our clinging to an idea of *what should be* rather than trying to *understand* what is.

In marriage more than in any other relationship the question of oscillation is more crucial. Over a certain number of years people undergo changes of many kinds, but because at a certain moment two individuals stood together on the same peak, we mistakenly believe they can always grow in the same direction.

Lawrence suggests a connection between man and woman based on an admission of two integrities, a recognition of ultimate independence.

In *Kangaroo* he observes the marriage of Jack and Victoria.

Jack is driving the car, and Victoria, sitting next to Somers, smiles at him. Jack is silent and unconcerned.

"Perhaps he knew his wife better than anyone else. At any rate he did not feel it necessary to keep an eye on her. If she liked to look at Somers with a strange, exposed smile, that was her affair. She could do as she liked in that direction, so far as he, Jack Callcott, was concerned. She was his wife: she knew it, and he knew it. And it was quite established and final. So long as she did not betray what was between her and him, as husband and wife, she could do as she liked with the rest of herself. And he could, quite rightly, trust her to be faithful to that undefinable relation which subsisted between them as man and wife. He didn't pretend and didn't want to occupy the whole field of her consciousness."

But of what, then, is it that this undefinable relation consists?

"It was something indefinite: *the field of contact* between their two personalities. Where their two personalities met and joined, they were one, and pledged to permanent fidelity. But that part in each of them which did not belong to the other was free from all enquiry or even from knowledge. Each silently consented to leave the other in large part unknown, unknown in word and deed and very being. They didn't want to know — too much knowledge would be like shackles... Such a marriage is established on a very subtle sense of honour and of individual integrity."

Lawrence-Somers is really very much disturbed by this wise arrangement. He is so truthful, always, that when he has finished describing it he tells us that Somers-Lawrence *is* disturbed, not liking the thought of applying the same philosophy to his own marriage. This is a human reaction to wisdom.

"But the day of the absolute is over." And yet there is between man and woman one connection which must be absolute. In *Kangaroo* Somers' wife Harriet is intuitively antagonistic to Somers' participation in the revolution; not so much in the participation as in his estrangement from her, his carrying *all* his energy, *all* his thought, and *all* his feeling into that new idea. What is she fighting for? She is sharp, and unrelenting. At first Somers is simply irritated, and terms the feelings of Harriet sheer interference, lack of understanding. Then thinking it over, she is partly right. And why?

"When a man and woman truly come together, when there is a marriage, then an unconscious vital connection is established between them like a blood-circuit. A man may forget a woman entirely with his head, and fling himself with energy and fervour into whatever job he is tackling, and all is well, all is good, *if he does not break that inner vital connection* which is the mystery of marriage. But let him once get out of unison, out of conjunction, let him inwardly break loose and come apart, let him fall into that worst of male vices, the vice of abstraction and mechanization, and have a concert of working alone and for himself, then he commits the breach. He hurts the woman, and he hurts himself, though neither may know why. A man must strive onward, but from the root of marriage... Like a tree that is rooted, always growing and flowering away from its root, so is a vitally active man. But let him take some false direction, and there is torture through the whole organism, roots and all. The *woman suffers blindly from the man's mistaken direction, and reacts blindly.*"

This time Harriet is right.

But there are times — and this is Lawrence's most frequent reproach — when woman does not understand the flowering away from the roots.

"The turning away from the personal life to the hateful male impersonal activity and shutting her out from this.

"Her greatest grief was when he turned away from their personal human life of intimacy to this impersonal business of male activity for which he was always craving.

"She emphatically opposed this principle of her externality. She agreed with the necessity for impersonal activity, but oh,

54

she insisted on being identified with the activity. And he insisted that it could not and should not be: that the pure male activity should be womanless, beyond woman. No man was beyond woman. But in his own quality of ultimate maker and breaker, he was womanless..."

There are many skirmishes between them. Somers wants to go out and "fight something with mankind."

" 'But what's your struggle for?' asks Harriet.

" 'I don't know. But it's inside me, and I haven't finished yet. To make some kind of opening — some kind of way for the afterwards... I intend to move with men and get men to move with me before I die.' "

"He had started off on his fiery course: always, as she said, to fall back, rather the worse for the attempt, on her. She had no use at all for fiery courses and efforts with the world of men. Let all that rubbish go."

He laughed, "realizing that most of what she said was true."

In love there must be resistance. "We ought to pray to be resisted and resisted to the bitter end." There must be resistance in relationships. It is the basis of strength, of balance, of unison.

* * *

Hierarchy. A hierarchy is a form, a formality. For the first time Lawrence insists on a form: there must be a hierarchy.

He uses the symbol of a boat in *Kangaroo*. The boat "Harriet and Lovat" is at sea. There must be a captain and there must be a crew. "We shall never sail any straight course at all until you realize that I am lord and master, and you my blissful consort," Somers tells Harriet.

Fortunately the whole voyage is made with a high sense of the comic — for after all, it is not fearfully important, and there are many women who could enjoy being the crew.

"And I want you to yield to my mystery and my divination, and let me put up my flag of a phœnix rising from a nest of flames..."

Harriet answers:: " 'Of course, you lonely phœnix, you are the bird, and the ashes, and the flames all by yourself!'

" 'Yes,' he said, 'you are the nest.' "

The reason why Harriet cannot quite believe in him as a captain is because he is: "not even really lord of his own bread and butter: next year they might both be starving. And he was not even master of himself, with his ungovernable furies, and his uncritical intimacies with people."

Further on Lawrence's truthfulness comes back, and he compromises: "Human love, human trust, are always perilous, because they break down. The greater the love, the greater the trust, and the greater the peril, the greater the disaster. Because to place absolute trust on another human being is in itself a disaster, both ways, since each human being is a ship that must sail its own course, even if it go in company with another ship."

So now we have not one ship and a captain, but *two ships,* two captains. For the sake of economy, it might be as well to have one ship and the two captains relieving each other on duty.

Of real importance (for after all, the matter of captains is secondary) is the *first choice,* and Lawrence points here to a frequent mistake: "We have made the mistake of idealism again. We have thought that the woman who thinks and talks as we do will be the blood-answer. And we force it to be so. To our disaster. The woman who thinks and talks as we do is almost sure to have no dynamic blood-polarity with us."

* * *

In *Kangaroo* Victoria is shown as an attractive feminine woman. What is the meaning of her? First she sees wonder in Somers. Faith, mere faith. This, at the moment when Harriet is showing too much critical intelligence, is particularly soothing. There is always the woman who will believe a man *absolutely*. There is always a fascinated woman, and a dissatisfied one. Lawrence is stating a fact.

Only by the exercise of extreme truthfulness does Somers extricate himself from the ointment-softness of Victoria's subjugation. He appreciates the high moment in Victoria, the Bacchic high moment which Somers, if he had had a true pagan heart, would have delected in. But he has not got a pagan heart, and the high moment of a flirt is, after all, transferable.

The understanding of Harriet is on another plane.

"She was too honest a female. She would know that the dishonour, as far as she felt it, lay in the desire, not in the act. For her too, honour did not consist in a pledged word kept according to pledge, but in a genuine feeling faithfully followed."

For this reason, perhaps, Harriet lasts through many books, and Victoria appears but once.

* * *

Androgynous writing. The intuitional quality in Lawrence resulted in a curious power in his writing which might be described as androgynous.

He had a complete realization of the feelings of women. In fact, very often he wrote *as a woman* would write. It is a well-known fact that a critic attributed *The White Peacock* to a woman.

In *Kangaroo* he describes the leader in this way: "Kangaroo wasn't really witty. But he had such an innocent charm, an extraordinary winsomeness, that it was much more delicious than wit" (to a woman). "His presence was warm" (this is also a feminine requisite, not usually a masculine one). "You felt that you were cuddled cozily like a child, on his breast, in the soft glow of his heart." (Again purely a woman's feeling.)

Lawrence either could feel such things, or, sitting next to Harriet, divine exactly what she was feeling and thinking about Kangaroo.

57

In *Women in Love* there is a description of a young man: "a soft, rather degenerate face... Its very softness was an attraction; it was a soft, warm nature, into which one might plunge with gratification." Also a feminine feeling.

What makes *Lady Chatterley's Lover* so remarkably complete as a love story is that there are consistently double points of view, and every moment of the relationship reveals the woman's feelings as well as the man's, and the woman's with the most delicate and subtle acuteness.

In small descriptions of clothes he does not see the woman's costume flatly, visually, as men do, but he is sensitive to the quality of materials, to the flow and suppleness, and intricacies of coloring. A hat has an angle, a certain mood, a class; so has the handling of an umbrella; so has the manner in which the dress is worn.

He is peculiarly aware of the very little occupations of women; how they handle babies; how they talk to them; how they cook; the various ways they have of setting a table, of serving tea; how they feel about a house, about furniture, about servants; how they go about cleaning... And there is never the feeling of an outsider, looking on at things which have no relation to him. Lawrence follows the current of small activities with a real revelation of the moods which accompany them.

Remember the aggressive house cleaning of Anna Brangwen before the tea party. Here there is an extreme, vivid reality in Lawrence. It made women sensitive to him, while at the same time they resented his reproaches. They felt that since he knew them, so intimately, so vulnerably, he should not have stood outside and criticized. He should have been forever and ever sympathetic.

At moments he was. His pity took the form of the most extraordinary tenderness. Mellors watching Lady Chatterley crying over the new born chicks because she wants a child — Mellors the very consistently manly man, is profoundly moved.

The blind reactions and sharpnesses of Harriet in *Kangaroo* move Somers. Lawrence does know, all the time, he does understand, but truth is far more important.

His botany is scientific knowledge, but his observation is feminine in its thoroughness and its sensitiveness. He knows the names of flowers, but he also senses differences between them besides the botanical.

In *Women in Love* the conversation between the two sisters at the very beginning of the book is strangely exclusive of any man-consciousness. They are talking about men, marriage, and children, but with a tacit, fundamental attitude exclusively feminine in a hard, lucid way.

Biologically it has been observed that a man's emotions are concentrated, while women's are spread all over their bodies. Somers in *Kangaroo* speaks of "feeling sensitive all over," and it may be that quality in Lawrence which makes him do that very special kind of writing which sometimes looks crinkled up with sensitiveness, almost bristling with it — like a woman's.

In all the descriptions of conflict the man and the woman's response is equally stated. He is absolutely conscious of the twofold currents, in even measures. There are no soliloquies. There is always a question and an answer.

His suspicion of the intellect is of course, close to the feminine nature. He confides in the intuition. He battles for the clairvoyance of it, through many chaotic pages. And this is purely a feminine battle. His moments of *blind* reactions strike a response in women.

Having touched the fundamental sources of woman's attitude and impulses, the rest would naturally follow. It is not the first time that artists and poets have come closer to the woman than other men have. But it is the first time that a man has so wholly and completely expressed woman accurately.

Language---Style---Symbolism

Lawrence's language makes a physical impression because he projected his physical response into the thing he observed. Watch him come into San Tomaso's Church: "I went into the Church. It was very dark... my senses were roused, they sprang awake in the *hot spiced darkness*. My skin was expectant, as if it expected some contact, some embrace, as if it were aware of the contiguity of the physical world, the *physical contact with the darkness* and the heavy suggestive substance of the enclosure. It was a thick, fierce darkness of the senses."

The elements of darkness and heat have passed into him through the senses, and are now one with the elements of the church.

He impels his poetic sensation to show itself in the actual description of the object. See how he writes of the sun in the story *Sun*: "She looked up through her fingers at the central sun, his blue pulsing roundness, whose outer edges streamed brilliance. Pulsing with marvellous blue, and alive, and streaming white fire from his edges, the sun!

"Meanwhile the clouds rose like white trees from behind the mountains, as the afternoon swooned in silence, rose and spread black branches quickly in the sky, from which lightning stabbed like birds." It is not the afternoon which swoons, but one's desire to swoon into the perfection of its silence, which Lawrence describes.

We have: "the exposed smile of Victoria" and "the exposed stare of Minette." These are not renderings of a physical fact, but of a sensation given by the nature of the smile and glance.

Such a handling of words is more familiar in poetry. Lawrence has transferred the qualities of poetry to his prose, even in many cases to the rhythm:

"Dark-eared asses and running men, running lads, twinkling donkeys ambling on fine little feet, under twin great baskets with tomatoes and gourds, twin great nets of bubble-shaped jars, twin bundles of neat-cut faggots of wood, neat as bunches of cigarettes, and twin net-sacks of charcoal. Donkeys, mules, on they come, great pannier baskets making a rhythm under the perched woman, great bundles bouncing against the sides of the slim-footed animals. A baby donkey trotting naked after its piled-up dam, a white, sandal-footed man following with the silent Indian haste, and a girl running on light feet."

Or: "The flesh neutralizing the spirit, the spirit neutralizing the flesh, the laws of the average asserted, this was the monks as they paced backwards and forwards."

Very often, in fact, it is the under-current of rhythm which makes the careless writing. The words almost cease to have a meaning; they have a cadence, a flow, and Lawrence gives in to the cadence. That is why there are so many "ands" and *enchaînements*, repetitions like choruses, words that are meant to suggest more than their own determinate, formal significance.

In language, too, Lawrence was prolific and varied. There is the almost classical simplicity of *Sons and Lovers*, the biblical flavour of *The Boy in the Bush*, the limpidity of *Twilight in Italy*, the tormented, inchoate opposition of words in *Women in Love* and *The Lost Girl* — he tormented words to catch the mobility of things, and sometimes their essencee, the quintessence of what they suggest. *Studies in American Classical Literature* is syncopated, with megaphonic insertions.

As pure descriptions the Dances in *Mornings in Mexico* are quite perfect. Here there is a rich objective vision, transfused by a fine poetic imagination. Sense of color, rhythm and form are keen, and so is the understanding of their symbolical significance. There is also an almost occult mesmerism in his rhythmic repetitions. They are too long to quote entirely and lose their continuity in extracts, but here are a few examples:

"Two men put on the eagle feathers and take the shield on their arm, and dance the pantomime of a fight, a spear dance. The rhythm is the same, really, the drum keeps up the heart-pulsation, the feet the peculiar bird-tread, the soft, heavy bird-like step that threads as it were towards the center of the earth...

"...The mystery of the wild creatures led from their fastness, their wintry retreats and holes in the ground, docilely fascinated by the delicacy and the commanding wistfulness of the maidens who went out to seek them, to seek food in the winter, and who draw after them, in a following, the wild, the timid, the rapacious animals... stepping behind the slow gyration of the two dark-fringed maidens, who shake their gourd rattles in a delicate, quick, three-pulsed rhythm... magical wistfulness of woman, the wonderful power of her seeking which can draw forth even the bear from his den..."

"Down, down, down they drop, on the heavy, ceaseless leap of the dance, and the great necklaces of shell-cores spring on the naked breasts, the neckshell flaps up and down, the short white kilt of woven stuff, with the heavy woollen embroidery, green and red and black, opens and shuts slightly to the strong lifting of the knees; the whitish cords that hang from the kilt-band at the side sway and coil forever down the side of the right leg, down to the ankle, the bells on the red-woven garters under the knees ripple without end, and the feet, in buckskin boots furred round the ankle black with a white tip, come down with a lovely, heavy soft precision, first one, then the other, dropping always plumb to earth..."

He is a painter; he has a keen faculty for distinguishing colors, their composition and alteration.

This quality of *color* in Lawrence's writing is very pronounced and subtly developed. He does a real painting of nature, animals, clothes, surroundings. Color never fails to appear. It is one of the things which give his work an incredible reality. In spite of the thought, the philosophy, the abstractions, his work is realistic because of the vividness of his senses. All his senses are acutely developed: scent, touch, sight, hearing, taste.

In *Mornings in Mexico* the earth is: "pallid with dryness inhuman, with a faint *taste* of alkali."

He has tried many times to express the texture of different skins, the chameleonesque qualities of eyes, the sensations given by the feel of sea water and rain on the body, the changes in the colors of the day. His sensorial penetration is complete. That is why his most abstract thought is always deep reaching: it is really concrete, it passes through the channels of the senses. Writing as a rule is characterized by either one quality or another. The intellectual dressing of abstractions is a familiar weakness of writers. But Lawrence worked like a painter who works on the anatomy, from which he paints the figure and over that the draperies.

This is also the cause for some phrases which have appeared ridiculous. Men and women in his books are conscious of each other's loins and hips, and of the movements of the body underneath the clothes. It is a familiar feeling to painters and sculptors, and in reality quite true, though as yet awkwardly expressed. Lawrence attempted some very difficult things with writing. For him it was an instrument of unlimited possibilities; he would give it the *bulgingness of sculpture,* the feeling of heavy material fulness: thus the loins of the men and women, the hips and buttocks. He would give it the nuances of paint: thus his effort to convey shades of color with words that had never been used for color. He would give it the rhythm of movement, of dancing: thus his wayward, formless, floating, word-shattering descriptions. He would give it sound, musicality, cadence: thus words sometimes used less for their sense than their sound. It was a daring thing to do. Sometimes he failed. But it was certainly the crevice in the wall, and opened a new world to us.

At a certain moment in *Women in Love* he indulges in the suggestivity created by the mixture of three languages. Gudrun and Loerke communicate by suggestion — not by the finished, chiselled product of one language but by the suggestivity of many languages.

Animals are brought in to make contrasts, or to help the visual image: we know how a rabbit eats, how a cat walks; we know the lightness of insects. Loerke's comprehension of Gudrun is insect-like. What else could give its delicacy and precision, its winged penetration of her?

He can make slow, limpid descriptions, and swift kaleidoscopic ones. He ranges from the impressionism of *The Lost Girl* to the Anglo-Saxon sobriety of *Reflections on the Death of a Porcupine*.

But his individuality is always bursting forth, always destroying any permanency, as if in suspicion of form. And then out he comes with slang, curses, trite phrases. He is full of surprises, of mischief; sometimes he shows bad taste. He is never monotonous or austere. Occasionally one feels he might have subdued his originality, but then we might have lost some of the vigor of his prose.

Even in his eccentricities he is rarely insincere. In most cases another word, or way of using the word, cannot be found. It corresponds perfectly to his own imagery, the fantastic mobility of his thought.

In his most careless pages there are evidences of his research. He had repudiated many old symbolic terms and had to create his own vocabulary. But when the old symbol corresponds to his thought he does use it, as he uses the worn phrases of the Bible.

He uses the very old symbol of the goose in his poetry. "And the Goose is the Bird of Heaven, a symbol of Yang, the highest creative energy, of love, constancy, truth, inspiration." (Ancient Pagan Symbols. Elizabeth Goldsmith.)

"...the intense potency of symbols is part memory..."

But it will not have *potency* if it is not truly remembered. The effort of memory is a kind of pilgrimage; the use of worn words to which there is no genuine reaction is like a senseless, unfelt, mechanical recitation of a rosary. Lawrence makes tremendous efforts to make a sincere pilgrimage, not to repeat mechanically anything of which the meaning has died for him.

He takes the old symbol of the swan and interprets it in the light of his own vision: the swan would be the vital flame, the pure animal spirit.

> "But he stoops, now
> in the dark
> upon us;
> he is treading our women
> and we men are put out
> as the vast white bird
> furrows out featherless women
> with unknown shocks
> and stamps his black marsh-feet on their white and
> marshy flesh."

Women are more closely bound to the earth. There is a secret, natural connection between them and elemental flows.

> "Come not with kisses
> not with caresses
> of hands and lips and murmurings;
> come with a hiss of wings
> and sea-touch tip of a beak
> and trembling of wet, webbed, wave-working feet
> into the marsh-soft belly."

There is an eager bowing towards the depths of the earth, in which we are to be renewed, for "when our eagerness leaves us, we are godless and full of thought."

"...Man is lop-sided on the side of the angels..."

The old symbol of the phœnix arises often in Lawrence's work, in *Kangaroo*, for instance. "The phœnix rises out of the ashes." It is the very image of his feelings on disintegration and resurrection. (See study of *Women in Love*.)

In the end Lawrence himself has pointed out the essence of his language, style and symbolism:

"When it comes to the meaning of anything, even the simplest word, then you must pause. Because there are two great categories of meaning, forever separate. There is mob-meaning and there is individual meaning. The word will take the individual off on his own journey, and its meaning will be his own meaning, based on his own genuine imaginative reaction. And when a word comes to us in its individual character and starts in us the individual response it is a great pleasure to us."

Over-Development

Lawrence concentrated on the pursuit of an experience with all the slow, intricate, laborious elements of his own nature. He grew within the novel, in a devious way which is the despair of the formalists. What he discovered in the multitudinous byways of his fancies and his intuitions was sometimes unessential, sometimes unique.

He was aware of infinite nuances, both of mood and of thought, and carried out their development relentlessly. The result was a fulness and expansiveness which was wearying to readers who had been brought up on direct, condensed, easily digested literature.

But we owe something to this over-development.

It is precisely by this shadowiness of outline, by his imprecision that Lawrence penetrated into the unknown. His eagerness to search out the hidden meaning in an ordinary event frequently led him to lavishness and excess in description. In this he sometimes resembles Marcel Proust. Layers of obscure memories were roused unexpectedly by the smell of a bun, or the lacing of a shoe. No one knew by what coordination a memory would rise out of oblivion and illumine the darkness of our world.

What is too simple and too direct leaves out a great deal.

Proust is meticulous. Lawrence sometimes progresses with the same infinite care.

Perhaps in a slight gesture, if we look at it closely ("the effort of attention"), there is the revelation of a symbol, the indication of a dream. Hence he dwells attentively on small things. He does not spare us in his books (particularly in *The Lost Girl*, and *Women in Love*) the long moments of his watchfulness, which often yield nothing. He is not chiselling to give us a work of formal art. He is living and progressing within his own book. Incidentally, he makes us live and progress by "an acceptance of the limitations of consciousness, and a leaning up against the sun-imbued world of chaos."

If we want to make the labyrinthian voyage — did we not make the labyrinthian voyage with Proust? — if we want to go along with him, very well. He is too busy, too intent, just now, to entertain us.

And very often an experience comes at the end of an unexpected turn, or yields its meaning only then. Look at his last book: *The Virgin and the Gypsy* (a book which convinces one that Lawrence's work was done when he died). It is only when we come to the last phrase: "*And only then she realized he had a name*," that we get the full shock of Yvette's unreal, transposed experience. The man without a name was a symbol of an almost impersonal experience of blood-life, in some way connected with the whole earth, with the universe rather than with a specific person. The man had never a name for her, as other people had. He had been a subterranean spark of livingness, come to rouse in her the dark gods, and then gone.

In Controversy

Certain of Lawrence's readers were so struck by the first wave of his sensuousness that they could go no further. No ideas, no poetry, no philosophy could exist outside of the appalling fact of "pornography." Lawrence, they said, was enslaved by sex. Meanwhile, *they* were smothered, overwhelmed, subjugated by sex. And here they remained, arguing in defense of purity, and against the slavery of sex — of Lawrence's slavery, I mean.

> "It is only immoral
> to be dead-alive
> sun-extinct
> and busy putting out the sun
> in other people."

This may not be an example of Lawrence's best poetry, but it is Lawrence's feeling about morality.

As to who was enslaved by sex, the man who could not see anything but sex in Lawrence, or Lawrence — ?

In explanation of his so-called morbidity it has also been said that the horror of war tortured Lawrence to such a degree that he sought an escape into sensuality, the "mindless sensuality" of *Women in Love.*

Lawrence's escape at that moment was a healthy instinct, which urges human beings towards life at the moment of death. Gerald is urged towards a blood-connection with Gudrun more keenly because of the death of his father. Lawrence reacted against war, which was death, with a passionate assertion of life. But as we will see, there was no "mindless sensuality" in *Women in Love*. (See study of *Women in Love*.)

* * *

A grave concern to healthy people who think morbidity is a contagious disease.

Of course there is morbidity of a kind in Lawrence. There is everything in Lawrence.

Every thinker has been in one sense morbid. Work or creation of any intensity has always produced a state of excessive sensibility. The trances of the Hindus, the exaltations of the Christian martyrs, the fever of creation and thought have all been equally abnormal. It was during such abnormal states that there appeared visions which were afterwards used by normal men in normal living.

Some of Lawrence's revolutionary, iconoclastic statements have given the impression that he was a mere anarchist. And in certain exasperated moments he was. Some of his reactions were excessive, for he was unhinged by the bitterness of his experiences. A great deal of rebellious, combative thought misses ultimate truth. Great writers have generally found themselves only when they have freed themselves of their antagonisms. Lawrence was never wholly free, but he found himself because he was strong enough to create poetry — poetry came first and rose above his anarchy.

But he was no mere scrapper. He was the only man who had the courage to fight the battle that we, ourselves, should fight against society — the eternal individual battle.

Some of his damnations, too, are to be read in the light of his ultimate purpose. Damning things and people was only the assertion of his spirit of independence from all prior thought. His right to assume such an attitude was justified by the absolute originality of his work.

There are two kinds of pity in Lawrence: one which is sub-ordinated to truth, the other which runs parallel with truth.

He seems to lack pity for the grey, tired city man, the sun-less one in *Sun,* and for Lady Chatterley's husband crippled in the war. But here he was not concerned with pity: it was subordinated to truth. In the work of other writers the be-trayed husband is made hateful so that feeling can go freely to the lovers. Lawrence would not have it so because it is not so. Feeling is all to be divided. Even within one love there is divided feeling; even within one truth there is divided dual truth. The two men in *England, My England!* are both dis-tressingly right, distressingly pitiable, one so responsible, the other so irresponsible, and both equally necessary, both harm-ful, both admirable. Lawrence never weighs. The poetry and the bare truth exist side by side. Pity wavers back and forth, just as ideas do, and convictions.

* * *

One word about influences, since no study is supposed to be complete without it.

Lawrence himself settled the question in his usual trenchant way in *Fantasia of the Unconscious:*

"I am not a proper archeologist, nor an anthropologist, nor an ethnologist. I am no scholar of any sort. But I am very grateful to scholars for their sound work. I have found hints, suggestions for what I say here in all kinds of scholarly books, from the Yoga and Plato and St. John the Evangel, and the early Greek philosophers like Herakleitos down to Fraser and his Golden Bough and even Freud and Frobenius. Even then I only remember hints — and I proceed by intuition."

He did appreciate Whitman's idea of the open road — his essential message. "The leaving of the soul free unto herself, the leaving of his fate to her and to the loom of the open road. Which is the bravest doctrine man ever proposed to himself.

Not by meditation. Not by fasting. Not by exploring heaven after heaven, inwardly, in the manner of the great mystics. Not by exaltation. Not by ecstasy. Not by any of these ways does the soul come into her own. Only by taking the open road. The soul living her life along the incarnate mystery of the open road..."

Whatever Lawrence owed to Hardy and Dostoevsky he transformed and recreated. Whatever influenced him served merely to illumine a part of his own self-contained world.

Twilight in Italy

A book to be considered by itself because it contains a Lawrence particularly true to himself. A book which cannot be read as an ordinary travel book, for Lawrence is again seeking the core of truth, and his voyage is philosophic, as well as a symbolic and sensuous one. Here he wanders as a creator at work.

He begins with a symbolical "way of the Cross" during which he speculates on the different aspects of the body according to the interpretations of different people. Christ on the Cross is altered each time by the vision of the carver.

"He has fallen forward, just dead, and the weight of the full-grown, mature body hangs on the nails of the hands... He is Death Incarnate. And the driver of the pack-horses acknowledges this deathly Christ as supreme Lord. The mountain peasant seems grounded upon fear, the fear of death, of physical death. Beyond this he knows nothing. His supreme sensation is in physical pain, and in its culmination..."

All along the road Lawrence feels that there is a kind of *worship of death*: "...the same neutral triumph of death, complete negative death, so complete as to be abstract, beyond cynicism in its completeness of *leaving off*."

One Christ is elegant, brave, keen. Death is important but it must be elegant. Another Christ is weak and sentimental. Self-pity has been expressed by the carver. Other people must have His death pictured with sensationalism, and much blood. Death for them is approached with violence.

73

At the end Lawrence reaches a moment of desolation before the last Christ because it represents the final denial of the body, such a complete surrender to death.

"It was one of old uncouth Christs hewn out of bare wood, having the long wedge-shaped limbs and thin flat legs that are significant of the true spirit, the desire to convey a religious truth, not a sensational experience... It had fallen on the naked living rocks.

"I wondered who would come and take the broken thing away, and for what purpose."

Lawrence himself was to come, "to preach the other half of the truth, Christ resurrected in the flesh." (See study of "The Religious Man.")

Lawrence also experiences the eternal desire of the poet in a moment of weariness "for *being*" rather than becoming, for motionlessness — the craving for finality.

So he stops in admiration of an old woman who is spinning, and closes his brain, silences the upper strata, and watches he with "the open eyes of the breast," seeing her with the vision of the body; and so he understands her. He broods then on the fact that though she does *not realize herself* she *possesses herself*, and wonders then if we cannot possess ourselves without consciousness. But it is precisely Lawrence's consciousness which makes him create the old woman for us. However, he is in the mood to rest from his individual consciousness.

At sunset, on the borderland of night Lawrence's consciousness reawakens to give him the meaning of his world in terms of day and night — day (the spirit, the positive, the eternal being) and night (the blood, the negative, the eternal non-being). In both night and day he had faith because he saw "the infinite in positive and negative." But in the midst of this contemplation he observes: "two monks walking in their garden, between the naked bony vines, walking in their wintry garden between the naked bony vines and olive trees." These monks, and the dimness of the twilight in which they paced backwards and forwards, become symbolical of the only state that Lawrence really despises — that which is neither positive nor negative, neither night nor day.

"Across, above them, was the faint, rousing dazzle of snow. They never looked up. But the dazzle of snow began to glow as they walked, the wonderful, faint, ethereal flush of the long range of snow in the heavens, at evening, began to kindle. Another world was coming to pass, the cold, rare night, it was *dawning* in exquisite icy rose upon the long mountain summit opposite. The monks walked backwards and forwards, talking, in the first undershadow.

"And I noticed that up above the snow, in the bluish sky, a frail moon had put forth, like a thin, scalloped film of ice floated out on the slow current of the coming night. And a bell sounded.

"And still the monks were pacing backwards and forwards, backwards and forwards, with the strange, *neutral regularity.*

"The shadows were coming across everything, because of the mountains in the west. Already the olive wood where I sat was extinguished. This was the world of the monks, the *rim of pallor between night and day.* Here they paced backwards and forwards, in the neutral, shadowless light of shadow.

"Neither the flare of day nor the completeness of night reached them, they paced the narrow path of the twilight, treading in the neutrality of the law. *Neither the blood nor the spirit spoke in them, only the law, the abstraction of the average. The infinite is positive and negative. But the average is only neutral. And the monks trod backwards and forwards down the line of neutrality.*

"Meanwhile, on the length of the mountain-ridge, the snow grew rose-incandescent, like heaven breaking into blossom. *After all, eternal not-being and eternal being are the same.* In the rosy snow that shone in heaven over a darkened earth was the ecstasy of consummation. *Night and day are one, light and dark are one, both the same in the origin and in the issue,*

both the same in the moment of ecstasy, light fused in darkness and darkness fused in light, as in the rosy snow above the
twilight."

This seeming paradox, that in the final analysis positive
meets negative, that eternal being and eternal not-being are
the same, in the origin and in the issue, as well as in *time,* is
one that has been the common property of all the great mystics,
though sometimes less clearly expressed The same paradox has
been restated in terms of modern science in the latest conclusions of Einstein. It remained for Lawrence, however, to give
mysticism a rebirth in terms which have the advantage both
over the traditional mysticism and the abstractions of mathe-
matics in that he made us feel the unity in this eternal paradox
through our senses. He restated mysticism in modern terms.

Women in Love

Women in Love is another interplay of relationships. Birkin is an almost direct projection of Lawrence's being.

Birkin appears at a wedding "dressed correctly for his part, yet there was an innate incongruity which caused a slight ridiculousness in his appearance. His nature was clever and separate, he did not fit at all in the conventional occasions. Yet he subordinated himself to the common idea, travestied himself." One can see that his incongruity in the conventional world is the measure of his fitness in one of abstract, individual values.

He "has no real critical faculty of people," says Gudrun of him. This trait reappears later in Somers, in *Kangaroo*, who "rushed into uncritical intimacies." A critical faculty is a kind of lucidity which arrests impulses. Birkin must have those blind impulses which make "failure a part of the living chaos."

His mistake was in choosing Hermione for a mistress. This caused a reaction which nearly prevented him from ever readjusting his values again We shall, however, consider Hermione more fully later on.

In Birkin "there was a great physical attractiveness — a curious hidden richness, that came through his thinness and pallor like another voice, conveying another knowledge of him. It was in the curves of his brow and chin, rich, fine exquisite curves, the powerful beauty of life itself."

He is often ill, and he had none of the actual physical richness of Gerald, the Hellenic statue.

But Ursula has already this "other knowledge of him" and

it is conveyed to us. He is the one who is physically rich, not Gerald.

Birkin has also the Lawrence mobility. The little Italian Countess at the house-party exclaims with the prerogative of the foreigner, in an imperfect but meaningful phrase: "Mr. Birkin, he is a changer." She has caught his chameleonesque character. It was the poet's habit to take moods and impulses seriously.

None of these are "qualities" of normal people. In normal people they would be considered faults. None of Lawrence's characters, in a way, can be understood without the artist-key. And by that I mean that Lawrence, being extremely personal, gave most of them the characters of creators, just as before I said that in extremes of emotion they were given the characters of poets. This is a clue to his characters. They are reflected fragments of him, the creator above all. As creators their variability, their complications, their questionings, their seekings, their analyses and thoughts are very natural. As normal people, no. But read them in terms of artists, and all is intelligible. Birkin is incongruous in the conventional world, but he is alive and powerful in another and more important world. His changeableness is the characteristic of the artist who dissolves all experience and gathers it together afterwards at the moment of creation. The mobility of Birkin amounts to a fault. See through Gerald's eyes: "he has a young, spontaneous goodness that attracted the other man infinitely, yet filled him with bitter chagrin, because he mistrusted it so much. He knew Birkin could do without him — could forget and not suffer." In normal life this is called fickleness. In the artist it is simply the instinct to absorb the essence of personalities and then pass on with what normally seems like a strange indifference.

Gudrun has the same temperament. Ursula and Gerald do not have it.

Birkin carries the burden of chaos; he struggles to extricate himself, but he is unable to do so by the same means as other people employ. In his relations with Ursula he makes her suffer for the "battle with his soul." The perpetual battle of Jack in *The Boy in the Bush* and later on, of Somers in *Kangaroo*: a struggle for *revaluations*. To Ursula, Birkin makes dishevelled statements, just as Somers will make later to Harriet.

He begins them with: "I don't know." Then he goes off into a kind of abstraction. Ursula reduces his phrases to simpler and less *exact* statements of his thought. Then he either gets angry, or gives up until he is able to restate them again himself more clearly. To him the visible is less important than the invisible, the unknown, the inarticulate.

It is not a struggle between him and Ursula but one of revaluations. "You and I," says Birkin, "let us begin at the beginning without jumping to conclusions." And he begins the slow, tortuous journey: "What are you? What am I? What is love? What is the center of our life?"

Poor Birkin. He makes many efforts. Every time he and Ursula talk together about his idea of love, or non-love, she ends by asking him if he does not love her, in a plain, direct way, and so he begins again: "What I want is a strange conjunction with you — not a meeting and mingling, but an equilibrium, a pure balance of two single beings — as the stars balance each other."

"Why drag in the stars," says Ursula.

Birkin: "Adam and Eve in the indestructible paradise, when he kept her single with himself, like a star in its orbit."

Ursula: "There you are — a star in its orbit — you the star — and you want a satellite — that's what *she* is to be! There — there — you've given yourself way! You want a satellite — Mars and his satellite — you've said it — you've dished yourself!"

In *Women in Love* Lawrence employs a method which was

to appear later in *Kangaroo*. He has created his Birkin (as later Somers) who carries the burden of Lawrence's earnestness, of his almost (to Ursula) ridiculous exaltations. And all the while Lawrence has also created the characters who *answer Birkin*, who state the other side of the case, who make him ridiculous, and who put him in the wrong.

Gudrun says: "But there are so many things in life that he simply doesn't know. Either he is not aware of their existence at all, or he dismisses them as merely negligible — things which are vital to the other person. In a way, he is not clever enough, he is too intense in spots."

Hermione says: "He lives an intensely spiritual life, at times, too, too wonderful. And then come the reactions. The violent and directless reactions between animalism and spiritual truths..."

It is the courageous truthfulness of Lawrence which is remarkable here, writing the two sides of the case, himself really seeking and wondering who is right, although it is so clear that he is Birkin, and also Somers in *Kangaroo*. However much he puts himself into his books, he is above all an artist since he can stand off from and observe critically even his most passionate feelings and convictions.

Hermione believed that she stood for spiritual truth. Lawrence is hard on Hermione, because she is one of the moderns who will warmth with their minds. Birkin is hard on her.

"Your passion is a lie. It isn't passion at all, it's your will. It's your bullying will. You want to clutch things and have them in your power... you haven't got any real body, any dark sensual body of life... only your lust to *know*."

Hermione has only *knowledge*, and, because of the knowledge, she thinks she is complete. The terrible thing in Hermione is her emptiness, her lack of centrality. Knowledge is on the outside, like a costume. But she is uncreative, not alone in art, but in livingness. Her love for Birkin is simply a desire for knowledge, which to her is power.

She comes into his rooms where he is busy copying a drawing of a Chinese goose:

" 'But why do you copy it,' she said, 'why not do something original?'

" 'I want to know it,' he replied. 'One gets more of China copying this picture than reading all the books.'

" 'And what do you get?' She was at once roused, she laid as it were violent hands on him, to extract his secret from him. She must know. It was a dreadful tyranny, an obsession in her, to know all he knew..."

Birkin turns to Ursula, who is soft, luxuriant, and very thoroughly woman, with a sensitive expectancy, a certain self-sufficiency in her warm livingness.

Ursula treats Birkin's ideas humorously but kindly enough. While the conversations last, the exchange of words, they only get more and more entangled. Ursula has no use for words. It is finally by a moment of surrender to the "dark gods" that they are united, more or less in disregard of Birkin's ideas. And his last phrase is still one of unsubdued complexity: "I wanted his (Gerald's) love too."

"But you can't have two kinds of loves," says Usula.

"I don't believe that," he answers.

GUDRUN AND GERALD—LOERKE

Gerald has "clear nothern flesh... gleaming beauty, maleness, like a young, good-humored, smiling wolf." He is "fair, sun-tanned, well made."

He is a "soldier, and an explorer, and a Napoleon of industry."

He has a great deal of "go," but as Gudrun observes, his "go" just goes to applying the latest appliances.

He is all for the outward world: he has a sense of class. And what does he live for? "To produce something tangible."

Birkin asks him: "Wherein does life center for you?"

"A far as I can make out it doesn't center at all. It is artificially held together by the social mechanism."

He has had mistresses, but has never really loved. Birkin suggests to him that the love of one woman might be the center of one's life. This is before he himself has found Ursula. Gerald is very doubtful.

When Gerald is mastering his Arab horse he does it with sheer brutality, and with physical power — nothing else. When Birkin, in one of his tirades, says the world is full of very nice, very rosy, healthy young men but that "their insides are full of ashes" it applies to Gerald. And why? Because there is a limitation in him, a strange emptiness. All his richness is on the outside. Sometimes he feels it. "He cast over in his mind what it would be possible to do, to save himself from the misery of nothingness, relieve the stress of his hollowness... there was nothing to do but bear the stress of his emptiness..."

Birkin at such moments means a great deal to him. He likes Birkin's fulness — just now it is a fulness of doubts, torments, hesitations, questionings, but it is a fulness. In him he finds the necessary *resistance,* which is as the basis of relationships. Their boxing together is very symbolical. Birkin is much stronger than Gerald had expected. They are realizing each other's strength, each other's presence through resistance — as we realize our own strength when it is pitted against an obstacle. There is pleasure in the physical struggle. It has another meaning too. They are mingling, physically — Birkin enjoys the beauty of Gerald. "We should enjoy everything," he says.

Slowly the thought of Ursula comes back to Birkin. And then they both talk about their ultimate desires — to be fulfilled in woman.

What is the first thing Gerald realizes about Gudrun? A propos of her staying away from a swimming party at Hermione's house, she makes an individualistic statement: "I won't bathe because I don't like the crowd."

"Whether he would or not she signified the real world to him. He wanted to come up to her standards, fulfill her expectations. He knew that her criterion was the only one that mattered. The others were all outsiders, instinctively, whatever they might be socially. And Gerald could not help it, he was bound to strive to come up to her criterion, fulfill her idea of a man and a human being."

He is making great concessions, the first one of class. Gudrun is a sculptress and an art teacher. She is also beautiful, soft-skinned, soft-limbed, confident, piquant, ironic. When the book begins she is discontented because: "everything fails to materialize."

From the very first moment, however, she "apprehends Gerald physically." His physical presence compels her, long before she is entirely aware of it, and long before she is clearly distinguished in his conscious world. There is a physical current. "She looked back at him with her fine blue eyes, and signalled full into his spirit..." And from then on there is an understanding between them.

But Gerald does not come wholly to her until the death of his father urges him blindly out of himself. There is no real love between them. If Lawrence had meant that we should abide by a "mindless sensuality" then the relationship between Gudrun and Gerald should have been quite perfect.

"He was not like a man to her, he was an incarnation, a great phrase of life... And she knew it was all no good, and that she would never go beyond him, he was the final approximation of life to her."

However, Gudrun was to go beyond Gerald, beyond the purely physical, to Loerke.

Ursula and Birkin are now married. Gudrun does not want to marry, neither does Gerald. The four of them go to the Tyrol mountains for a holiday.

Birkin is now solved in his love for Ursula. But it is not

an absolute solution. It is not the ultimate, satisfactory relationship. In a way, in the way of ideas, Birkin is slightly defeated, although he is very happy, and loves Ursula deeply. So now Lawrence leaves him to his half-solution, and transfers himself to Loerke.

Loerke is an artist, a sculptor. He and Gudrun talk about their work and art. "They had a curious game with each other, Gudrun and Loerke, of infinite suggestivity, strange and leering, as if they had some esoteric understanding of life, that they alone were initiated into the fearful central secrets, that the world dared not know. Their whole correspondence was in a strange, barely comprehensible suggestivity...

"It was curious what a sense of elation and freedom Gudrun found in this communication."

Meanwhile Gerald sees in Loerke only a puny, unprepossessing foreigner and cannot understand what makes Gudrun take an interest in him. He has none of the physical nobility, pride, and masterfulness of Gerald.

But Loerke: "can touch the quick of her... with the fine insinuating blade of his insect-like comprehension of her."

Gerald has penetrated all the *outer* places of Gudrun's soul. Gerald represents the man's world — the outside. There remains in Gudrun, as in the "Princess" an untouched core, something as yet unsatisfied. Her mind and Loerke's were set in the same kind of activity: they were craftsmen, and they lived outside of ordinary standards and common desires. Loerke almost disregards Gudrun's beauty as Birkin had almost disregarded Ursula's. "You are beautiful, and I am glad of it. But it isn't that. It is that you have a certain wit, it is a kind of understanding... I am waiting the match to my particular intelligence."

In both there is non-conformity.

When they go out together: "they spend much time... laughing in an endless sequence of quips and jests and polyglot fancies. The fancies were the reality to both of them, they were both happy, tossing about the coloured balls of verbal humour and whimsicality. Their natures seemed to sparkle in full interplay, they were enjoying a pure game..."

Neither Gudrun nor Gerald are in love with each other, and yet Gerald will not relinquish his physical possession of her.

He comes upon Gudrun and Loerke out on the snow and uses violence on both of them, wishing blindly to kill them, leaving Gudrun half-strangled on her knees, Loerke also thrown on the ground. Then he goes off in a daze, walks until he is worn out, sinks in the snow and dies. So it is Gerald who dies, not Loerke. It is the "mindless sensuality" which dies. Yet it has been said that Lawrence in *Women in Love* had urged us to mindless sensuality and disintegration.

The talk of disintegration here, as in other books, appears at first baffling, a contradiction to Lawrence's creativenesss.

Gudrun and Loerke's minds both believe: "there was only the inner, individual darkness, sensation with the ego, the obscene religious mystery of ultimate reduction, the mystic frictional activities of diabolical reducing down, disintegrating the vital organic body of life..."

The sensation of decay often appears in Lawrence's characters. Birkin has written his bohemian friends a letter which they ridicule. "And in the great retrogression, the reducing back of the created body of life, we get knowledge, and beyond knowledge the phosphorescent ecstasy of acute sensation..."

This is the same thing which he described in his poetry. Man goes through phases of livingness and phases of death. That is part of the continuous renewal, and becoming. It is a *transcendent experience*, symbolical of our continuity of life; we are born and die, we are born and die, as often as we have the vitality to be born again; and this movement is not confined to the hours between our physical birth and our physical death. It is an evolution of the mind and soul within themselves, the evolution of the universe reduced to the terms of our own souls.

Scientists and philosophers who have gathered up all the observed facts about the life of man, and of the earth, stars and planets, and their laws, have told us that birth, life, disintegration, and renewal, is the cycle of the universe. But they were looking *out* from themselves; if they had looked *into* themselves they would have observed the same cycles, as Lawrence did. Lawrence was not interested in the cosmos, and it is a mistake to read his books as great cosmic allegories. He was not interested in God in the abstract but in the gods that inhabited Somers' body (in *Kangaroo*) and that were his personal and individual possessions. Thus Lawrence reduced his universe strictly to what he felt and experienced in himself, but, precisely because he was so intensely personal, that reduced universe is as full and complete as any conceived by cosmic minds. Within the limits of this personal universe, then, by inward contemplation, he discovered the personally experienced cycle of birth, life, disintegration and renewal.

Lawrence's experience of disintegration of the soul, and its meaning for him is also described in his essay on "Edgar Allan Poe." "Poe had a pretty bitter doom. Doomed to seethe down his soul in a great continuous convulsion of disintegration and doomed to register the process. And then doomed to be abused for it, when he had performed some of the bitterest tasks of human experience that can be asked of man. Necessary tasks too. *For the human soul must suffer its own disintegration, consciously, if ever it is to survive.*"

Fantasia
of the Unconscious

Just as in *Studies in Classical American Literature* Lawrence brought his entire individual philosophy to bear upon criticism, so in considering psychology he had to give us a personal interpretation. There is no application of psychological formulas in his novels, but rather an attempt to transcend them. "Commandments should fade as flowers do..." Formulas should allow ample room for the unexpected, for "the creative powers and impulses of men."

In handling the psychological abstractions Lawrence had also to strike at a vital truth.

He expressed the protest of the individual imagination against automatic conclusions — against the danger of automatic pigeonholing.

He expressed the instinct that there was a moment for clarity, the utmost clarity, but also a refuge from clarity in his favorite "darkness," the yet unrevealed, the still *living mystery.*

Science, he thought, was in danger of raising consciousness to a mob-meaning. Which would make the unconscious another mass production on sale anywhere, and which anyone could memorize. Thus there would again be no escape. *There would be formulas, to which individuals would stick until the formula had died, instead of there being individuals who would create each one his own living formulas — each for himself,* like the gods who multiplied so that there could be gods enough to satisfy each man.

Religion and idealism had said: You should do this or that, because it is according to the highest concept of living we know.

Lawrence feared that psychology would soon say: A hundred cases have proved that the reason why you do this or that falls under such and such a category, and requires such a cure. It is in the catalogue.

Lawrence with his usual flair, again sensed the intellect, that adroit juggler, at his adroit job.

This is one example of Lawrence's method of reasoning against reasoning. For instance: "There is an automatic-logical conclusion in the psyche, as there is in the mind." So much for the fact.

But Lawrence grants the soul a horror of *automatism*.

"While the soul really lives, its deepest dread is perhaps the dread of automatism. For automatism in life is a forestalling of the death process."

Suppose that psychology contends that a certain incest dream is a wish-fulfillment. According to Lawrence: "an incest dream would not prove an incest desire in the living psyche. Rather the contrary, a living fear of the automatic conclusion: the soul's just dread of automatism. That which is lovely (and current) to the automatic process is hateful to the *spontaneous soul*."

So Lawrence hands us back a spontaneous soul, which can even free itself of certain psychological automatic-logical conclusions.

Kangaroo

In *Kangaroo* one comes unawares upon an undiluted Lawrence. Due perhaps to pessimism and depression at the time, caused by the war, his inventive faculties are less in evidence. In other books there was always a mixture of invention and reality. But in *Kangaroo* Lawrence projected himself into Somers — more than he did in Birkin, and more than later on in Mellors.

First of all there is the physique: Somers was labelled as unfit during the examinations for conscription. " 'Let them label me unfit,' he said to himself. I know my own body is fragile, in its way, but it is also very strong, and it's the only body that would carry my particular self.' "

"Somers... just looked a foreign sort of little bloke — but a gentleman. The chief difference was that he looked sensitive all over, his body, even its clothing, and his feet, even his brown shoes all equally sensitive with his face."

This is in contrast with Jack who "seemed strong and insensitive in the body, only his face vulnerable. His feet might have been made of leather all the way through, tramping with an insentient tread. Whereas Somers put down his feet delicately, as if they had a life of their own, mindful of each step a contact with the earth."

There is Somer's talk which is Lawrence: "When Somers was talking and telling it was fascinating, and his quick, mobile face changed and seemed full of magic. Perhaps it was difficult to locate any definite Somers, any one individual in all this ripple and animation and communication. The man himself seemed lost in the bright aura of his rapid consciousness."

Lawrence had given many of his characters his thoughts and his feelings, but mixed with others. In Somers there is little alteration. Unconsciously, he has passed into him almost completely.

Somers had the same "sauvagerie" as Lawrence had about neighboring: "it was usually the same. He started by holding himself aloof, then gradually he let himself get mixed in, and then he had revulsions."

And here is at last a very clear statement of the "class" problem for Lawrence. The story has developed from the arrival of Harriet and Richard Somers in a new country, Australia, to the "neighboring" with Jack and Victoria Callcott. There is a difference between them which is difficult to analyze. They are having tea together for the first time.

"Somers was of the people himself, and he had that alert instinct of the common people, the instinctive knowledge of what his neighbor was wanting and thinking, and the instinctive necessity to answer. With the other classes, there is a certain definite breach between individual and individual, and not much goes across except what is intended to go across (this is what we call tact). But with the common people... there is no breach. The communication is silent and involuntary, the give and take flows like waves from person to person, and each one knows, unless he is foiled by speech." (This is the sincerity of the people who have not learned enough language to disguise themselves with.)

"And as for the two men: Somers seemed a gentleman, and Jack didn't want to be a gentleman. Somers seemed a real gentleman. And yet Jack recognized in him at once the intuitive response which only subsists, normally, between members of the same class: between the common people... The one thing which Somers had kept, and which he possessed in a very high degree was the power of intuitive communication with

90

others. Much as he wanted to be alone, to stand clear from the weary business of unanimity with everybody, he had never chosen really to suspend this power of intuitive response..."

Lawrence did say in the *Autobiographical Sketch* that he suffered because: "I cannot make the transfer from my own class into the middle class."

In spite of the friendliness of people, of his innate aristocracy, of his feelings for his own class, of the understanding, there is a certain isolation. But it is not due to class. "Why is there so little contact between myself and the people whom I know? Why has the contact no vital meaning?"

He puts it all down to class divisions, himself, but it is not so. He is deluded by the inordinate class distinctions existing in England, which do form a real blind barrier between men. But it is easy to see that he is isolated simply because he is an individualist and a creator. Such a man, even in European countries where there are no class distinctions for artists, still feels isolation. In Latin countries the artist enjoys a distinction in all classes. Not so in England. But Lawrence would always have remained apart in any country. He was of no class. He was uniquely himself. He did not know it, but *he was making a class for himself*, for others somewhat like him.

Lawrence continues to be so vividly himself in Somers that he even includes his own objections to himself, his admissions of mistakes, or of indecisions. It is Harriet who is spokesman for this anti-Lawrence expression. Through her he states the other side of the case, *the side he often agrees with against himself*. He is always truthful. " 'I am a fool,' said Somers, which is the most frequent discovery he ever made. It came moreover, every time with a new shock of surprise and chagrin. Every time he climbed a new mountain range and looked over, he saw, not only a new world, but a big anticipatory fool on this side of it, namely, himself."

Of course, he is obliged to say that because he has put all of himself, undisguised, and without much selection, into his novel. If he is to put all his moods down, some of them will forcibly need to be damned. But all these moods, damnable or not, are spontaneous and interesting, and *Kangaroo* is valuable.

Kangaroo begins at first with little "élan." Before Lawrence begins to create again after the experience of the war, he is making his own literal preparations, which are a kind of wistful statement of facts. So *Kangaroo* begins quietly, untransformed. Lawrence has been oppressed by the war, he is taking stock, wonderlessly. There is a great difference between his first description of Australia and those in *The Boy in the Bush* later, where eagerness is again in full sail.

The wonder is momentarily still. The descriptions are rather enumerative. Cottages, sea, stores, events, neighbors. It makes one think of the whole class of authors who think that taking an inventory of the universe is really literature.

Lawrence has quite definitely a feeling of freedom. But there is an emptiness about this freedom. He is in the unillumined chaos. He says so himself: "Poor Richard Lovat wearied himself to death struggling with the problem of himself and calling it Australia."

And because of his devotion to conflict, he finds "accomplished liberty hopelessly uninteresting."

"The absence of inner meaning," which is in Australia, is for the moment in a pessimistic Lawrence.

Just then events begin to enmesh him; he is offered a participation in rather vital activities in the shape of a revolutionary movement, and his enthusiasm is expected. "But, alas, it was just too late. In some strange way Somers felt that he had come to the end of transports; they had no more mystery for him; at least not this kind; or perhaps no more charm. Some bubble or other had burst in his heart. All his body and fibres wanted to go over and touch the other great being (Kangaroo, the leader) into a storm, a response. But his soul wouldn't. The coloured bubble had burst."

But this is only a manner of speaking. I have said that

Lawrence always surrendered to experience; his creativeness urged him to do so. Here he *appears* to hold back. He is told that he is holding back. He does not go through the experience of revolution with Kangaroo. But that is only a way of speaking. *What is going through an experience?* Sometimes it is living it out in action, but *sometimes it is denying it.* That is one kind of experience. Lawrence does not take part in the revolution, but he takes part in a terrific struggle with himself. The true experience here was whether or not to amalgamate with Kangaroo. To withhold, and to let the experience die, and lie there is one thing. But to withhold because of a profounder inner revolution is to deny one experience for another of greater importance, that is all. Lawrence holds back from the revolution, but fearlessly starts another *bloody one within himself.*

Kangaroo is the journal of this struggle. That is why he says later: "'Chapter follows chapter, and nothing doing. But man is a thought-adventurer, and his falls into the Charybdis of ointment, and his shipwrecks on the rocks of ages, and his kisses across chasms, and his silhouette on a minaret: surely these are as thrilling as most things."

More thrilling than the revolution. "Somers was silent, very much impressed (by Kangaroo, the leader), though his heart was heavy. Why did his heart feel so heavy? Politics — conspiracy — political power; it was all so alien to him. Somehow in his soul he always meant something quite different, when he thought of action along with other men."

At the same time he thinks that it was his own high destiny to be a leader.

It was, but in a very different kind of revolution, an equally thrilling and more enduring one.

But why should this inner revolution be so agonizing? Because it is all to be accomplished by instinct and vision.

What has he got against the leader? " 'I want to hear,' said Kangaroo, 'your case against me.'

" 'It's not a case, Kangaroo,' said Richard, 'it's a sort of instinct.' "

What a task — to make an instinct clear to the mind!

People in the throes of an instinct are tormented by a peculiar distemper, restlessness, blackness. An intuition cannot be explained rationally either to others or even to one's self. Women know the despair. It is often the cause of hysterics, tears, unreasonableness. The instinct is there: sometimes even to justify it, in a frantic effort to give a rational explanation, one is invented, which adds to the confusion. Lawrence did not invent explanations. He stuck to the inarticulate instinct; but he suffered. He was bewildered and sick with himself. It is not only Harriet's patience which is worn thin, but his own: "There is no arguing with the instinctive passionate self."

The inner revolution, substituted for Kangaroo's, becomes tremendous. The tenseness of certain chapters is like that of a nightmare.

Lawrence's intuition was right. But before he is sure of it, he has tortured Kangaroo, and his wife, and his neighbors, and himself.

And all the while, what is the reason for Lawrence's complication-producing mechanism? It is the business of the creator. He was to write precisely this book *Kangaroo, a reflection of all such complications*. Other men overtaken by the same spirit of intuition could then clarify this intuition and be spared much of the revolution. The madness of Lawrence was to set a precedent, so that other people might realized the sanity of their own feelings, proved by the conclusions of *Kangaroo*.

Poor Somers is just as tired as we are. In the eighth chapter he registers a new vow; not to take things with too overwhelming an amount of emotional seriousness, but to accept everything that comes along with a certain sang-froid and not to sit frenziedly in judgment before he has heard the case.

It is fortunate that the vow only comes in the eighth chapter, or we should not have learned that revolutions are better inwardly fought in ourselves than *en masse*. The masses can throw bombs, but they cannot create a soul.

Lawrence is always getting entangled, and weary of his entanglements. There is nothing more discouraging, more ungrateful, than a truth perceived by intuition. Over and over again he struggles to formulate it, and has to acknowledge that he cannot; has to accept the chaos. When the emotional vulnerability reaches a climax, almost a madness, he takes refuge in nature. He goes to the sea.

"And there, with his hands in his pockets, he drifted into indifference." (Kangaroo is dying.) "The far off, far off, far off indifference... as if he had landed on another planet, as a man might land after death. Leaving behind the body of care. Even the body of desire. Shed. All that had meant so much to him, shed. All the old world and self of care, the beautiful care as well as the weary care, shed like a dead body. 'What have I cared about? What have I cared for? There is nothing to care about. Why do I wrestle with my soul? I have no soul.'"

But this is "only the great pause between carings."

Before that, the demon that was in him! A demon of activity, cursed with restlessness, always effervescent, always *seeking* difficulties, perversely, says Harriet! Lawrence has given Somers the devil of the creator — his own devil! It is a force which is always exploding and *seeking to explode*. At best it is a self-created stimulation which allows no moment of peace. It is a seething, and an evasion of peace. Creators know it. "All is well with the world," says Harriet; "come in to tea." But the devil is loose. It upheaves the crust of contentment, of apparent well being, and chooses the chaos. For in the chaos there is life, dark life to be illumined with visions. "Everything is wrong with the world," says the devil in the creator. "I cannot come to tea until I have mastered the chaos."

And at certain moments he is "a sort of human bomb, all black inside, and primed; I hope the hour and place will come for my going off; for my exploding with the maximum amount of havoc. Some men have to be bombs, *to explode and make breaches in the walls that shut life in.*"

Lawrence has gone off, many times.

In the story there is a real bomb, thrown at a revolutionary meeting. There is also Lawrence the human bomb. He is the leader of his own revolution — of ideas.

The meeting of Somers and Kangaroo is awesome; two kinds of powers.

Kangaroo is Jewish with "the very best that is in the Jewish blood: a faculty for pure disinterestedness and warm, physically warm love... and a Jehovah-kindliness." But also: "the shrewd fiendish sublety of will. He loves mankind with a big, impersonal fire." A generous, passionate man, who believed in the inspirational force of love.

Somers: "I don't quite believe that love is the one and only exclusive force or mystery of living inspiration." And he goes off into rather obscure mysticism and metaphysics. Kangaroo cannot follow him.

We have to coordinate all we know to sense that Lawrence means it is the phallic which is the other and deeper force. But Kangaroo protests: "Aren't you merely inventing other terms for the same thing that I mean and that I call love?"

And Somers is silent.

"So again came back to him the ever recurring warning that some men must of their own choice and will listen only to the living life that is a rising tide in their own being, and listen, listen, listen for the injunction, and give heed and know and obey all they can. Some men must live by this *unremitting inwardness,* no matter what the rest of the world does. They must not let the rush of the world's outwardness sweep them away: or if they are swept away they must struggle back."

Kangaroo is given to a kind of cosmic love somewhat like Whitman's. Somers is suspicious of cosmic love. For creation begins and ends at the core of individuality and it is only by merging into art (like the sum total of Lawrence's work) that it goes to serve the universe.

The death of Kangaroo reveals a strange scene.

"Say you love me," pleads Kangaroo.

"No," answers Somers, "I cannot say it." He could not say it in Kangaroo's sense of the word; he was being obstinately true to his meaning of the word. In Kangaroo's sense he did not love him. In his own, perhaps. There is nothing monstrously inhuman in this symbolic scene: Somers' loyalty to his own soul is tested.

Somers had been swept away by the greatness of Kangaroo, who has been superb, appealing, convincing, in his own sincerity.

But Lawrence "must live by this unremitting inwardness and so must struggle to take himself back.

"'Who is it that you feel you are with, beside me — or feel themselves with you?' Harriet was asking.

"'No one.'"

Kangaroo was outwardly and in his way, heroic.

Lawrence is inwardly, in his own way, more heroic.

Kangaroo had followers.

Lawrence had no one.

The Poet

In considering Lawrence's poetry it is necessary to set to one side that part which is merely expository and didactic, where he was repeating ideas better expressed in his prose and belonging more properly to prose, as distinct from the relatively few poems in which the true poet in him spoke naturally and spontaneously. Lawrence himself recognized that this separation was necessary when he wrote in *Chaos in Poetry*: "The suffused fragments are the best, those that are only comprehensible with the senses, with a vision passing into touch and sound, then again touch and the bursting of a bubble of an image."

It is impossible, even if it were necessary, to criticize these "suffused fragments." Edward Titus in his "Criticism of Poetry" *(This Quarter)* has stated clearly the nature of the difficulty: "Stated summarily, poetry, as we conceive it, by its nature, does not lend itself to criticism. Poetry may be sung, it may be read silently or aloud; poetry may be dreamed, it may be lived, laughed, loved or hated; it may be discussed as one would a pleasant or unpleasant experience; it may be treated with indifference, liked or disliked or ignored, it may or may not be a stimulus, but one may as well bay at the moon as criticize it."

This particularly applicable to the group of poems entitled *Creatures* in *Birds, Beasts and Flowers*. For here there is not only acute observation of nature but a strange penetration into and identification with the life and world of animals. Evidences of Lawrence's gift for projecting himself into nature were not lacking in his prose. One has only to remember that passage in *Women in Love* where Gudrun is watching the water plants: "But she could feel their turgid, fleshly structure as in a *sensuous vision,* she knew how they rose out of the mud, she knew how they thrust out from themselves, how they stood stiff and succulent against the air."

In the same manner Lawrence, in these poems, closes all his human senses, in order to live for one moment in the senses of the animal whose world he enters. He does not attribute human feelings to animals as sentimental poets have been in the habit of doing, but the feelings he conceives to be their own, and which have little or no connection with ours. In the *Fish* for example, we are not merely *looking* at fish, or it would be "silvery," "swimming" or "sleeping." We are by a kind of magic shedding our human feelings like a costume, to enter that most foreign of foreign worlds — the world of the fish:

"Aqueous, subaqueous,
Submerged
And wave-thrilled.

As the waters roll

Roll you.
The waters wash,
You wash in oneness

And never emerge.

Never know,
Never grasp.

Your life a sluice of sensation along your sides,
A flush at the flails of your fins, down the whorl of
        your tail,
And water wetly on fire in the grates of your gills;
Fixed water eyes."

This is as wordlessly suggestive as music, as for example the "Poisson d'Or" of Debussy.

> "To sink, and rise,
> And go to sleep with the waters:
> . . . .
> Loveless and so lively!"

Slowly he realizes that in the "feelingless" life of the fish there is another world:

> "I didn't know his God,
> . . . .
> I am not the measure of creation.
> . . . .
> His God stands outside my God.
>
> And the gold-and-green pure lacquer mucus comes off
>   in my hand,
> And the red-gold mirror-eye stares and dies,
> And the water-suave contour dims.
>
> But not before I have had to know
> He was born in front of my sunrise,
> Before my day."

Here it is almost as if he were in a trance in which he communicates with another plane of existence. Approaching with wary sensitivity he leaves us with a completely objective image:

> "No fingers, no hands and feet, no lips;
> No tender muzzles,
> No wistful bellies,
> . . . .
> ...they swarm in companies
> But soundless, and out of contact.
> A magnetism in the water between them only.
> . . . .
> And their pre-world loneliness,
> And more-than-lovelessness,
> They move in other circles."

He shows the same acute observation when he watches a baby tortoise:

"To take your first solitary bite
And move on your slow, solitary hunt.
Your bright, dark little eye,
Your eye of a dark disturbed night,
Under its slow lid, tiny baby tortoise,
So indomitable.

Do you wonder at the world, as slowly you turn your
   head in its whimple,
And look with laconic, black eyes?
Or is sleep coming over you again,
The non-life?"

The "non-life" of certain animals fascinates Lawrence. "Non-life" as compared particularly with our life of the mind and its activities but life on another perhaps dimly remembered plane which it is strange to reenter through Lawrence.

"Fulfilled of the slow passion of pitching through
   immemorial ages
Your little round house in the midst of chaos."

Just as he resurrected the ancient cult of phallic worship, so he resurrects other forgotten worlds buried in our memories. As in the *Hummingbird*:

"I can imagine, in some other world
Primeval-dumb, far back,
In that most awful stillness, that only gasped and
   hummed,
Humming-birds raced down the avenues."

The snake "comes from the burning bowls of the earth." And the ass:

"His big, furry head,
His big, regretful eyes,
His diminished, drooping hindquarters,
His small toes
. . . .
He regrets something that he remembers."

101

In poems of lesser quality Lawrence fails to remain within the world of nature. Too often he uses animal life or nature to illustrate some human principle or emotion. And then worlds and metaphors are mixed, his plants and animals loose their identities, and his abstractions are made no clearer. Poetry as distinguished from prose is essentially that moment of ecstasy, like a moment in music, in which senses and imagination fuse and flame. Lawrence had many such moments but not all of them reached that white heat of fusion. Of course as ideas they are always interesting and revealing, but he usually expressed them more fittingly in his prose.

That Lawrence was, however, quite capable of fusing his philosophic ideas in poetry is shown in the poem *New Heaven and Earth*. Nowhere in his prose did Lawrence reach out further mystically, and at the same time the poem itself sustains throughout a fittingly high note and a deep rhythmic undercurrent, rising to a climax when he enters and possesses the "unknown world."

The poem begins with a simple description of his "old world," the everyday world of which he had been too much a part:

"I was so weary of the world,
I was so sick of it,
Everything was tainted with myself,

. . . .
...it was all tainted with myself,
I knew it all to start with
Because it was all myself."

He had reached the extreme of self-consciousness:

"When I gathered flowers, I knew it was myself
plucking my own flowering."

Living that everyday life, letting his mind associate and merge with the world's mind and its activities, he realizes that he had become an inseparable fragment of that world. So long as he should identify himself with that world he was responsible of it; all was in him, and he in all. He was its creator until he should create something new. This is a recurrence of Lawrence's idea, with which we are already familiar, of the evolution of the universe reduced to terms of our individual souls:

> "When I saw the torn dead I knew it was my own
>   torn dead body
> It was all me, I had done it all in my own flesh.
> . . . .
> I was the God and the creation at once;
> Creator, I looked at my creation;
> Created, I looked at myself, the creator."

So the creator must die, he must bury himself, which was his world, his creation. Here follows inevitably the process of disintegration which Lawrence believed was a part of the cycle through which each soul must pass to reach life.

> "At last came death, sufficiency of death,
> And that at last relieved me, I died.
> . . . .
> Dead and trodden to naught in the sour black earth
> Of the tomb; dead and trodden to naught, trodden to
>   naught."

And so he comes to the eternal non-being, which, as he has said in *Twilight in Italy*, is the same as eternal being: the seeming paradox that in the final analysis positive meets negative, that eternal being and eternal non-being are the same in the origin and in the issue, that has been the common property of all the great mystics.

> "For when it is quite, quite nothing, then it is
>   everything;
> When I am trodden quite out, quite, quite out,
> Every vestige gone..."

At that moment when the world died in him and he with it, at that moment he rose:

"Risen, and setting my foot in another world
Risen, accomplishing a resurrection..."

And so he discovers a new world:

"...that which was verily not me...
. . . .
It was the unknown."

New Heaven and Earth is an allegory of Lawrence's wide cycle of experience. Widening and widening the boundaries of experience and understanding he inevitably reached the breaking point in his own disintegration through which in turn he touched the secret mysteries of the earth and so found new sources of strength and deeper life:

"The unknown, strong current of life supreme
Drowns me and sweeps me away and holds me down
To the sources of mystery, in the depths,
Extinguishes there my risen resurrected life
And kindles it further at the core of utter mystery."

The Princess

The Princess is the fairytale of mysterious individuality. When her father says to her: "People and the things they say and do... it is all nothing. Inside everybody there is another creature, a demon which doesn't care at all. You peel away the things they say and do and feel... And in the middle of everybody there is a green demon which you can't peel away. And this green demon never changes, and it doesn't care at all about the things that happen to the outside leaves of the person...

"And that is why you will never care for any of the people in the world very much. Because their demons are all dwindled and vulgar." The poor little Princess is vowed to reticence, "the impossibility of intimacy."

"She was the Princess, and sardonically she looked out on a princeless world..."

She was in a way that scentless, exquisite, rootless mysticism that Lawrence did not believe in. She should, according to Lawrence's philosophy, soon die. Her detachment was sacred, but also mortal.

She is left alone in the world when her father dies. She goes travelling through New Mexico. A ride is arranged for her and a friend, with Romero as a guide. Romero is a Mexican who interests the Princess. During the ride one of the horses is hurt. The friend, Miss Cummins, turns back home. The Princess and the guide continue and reach a summit.

105

There has been an attraction between them, but when Romero takes advantage of it and forces her will to possess her, and does possess her physically, he cannot *conquer her*. Why cannot he conquer her? Because of the demon which you can't peel away... the real self which does not care what happens to its outer leaves.

Romero is violent with the Princess, but she does not submit, and she does not die. Lawrence's philosophy does not interfere. He is telling about the *mystery* of individuality...

Lady Chatterley's Lover

In *Lady Chatterley's Lover* Lawrence's work reaches its climax. Paradoxically it is at once his fleshliest and his most mystical work. Artistically it is his best novel because one idea is sustained to its conclusion with intensity and clarity. Struggle and chaos had burned themselves out in the earlier novels and for the first time Lawrence could, in Walter Pater's words: "burn with a pure white flame." The result is our only complete modern love story.

To the telling of this story he brought the combined forces of his sensuous grasp of reality and his poetic symbolism. With the symbolism he expressed conceptions too subtle to reach the intellect directly. I do not refer to the obvious symbolism of Clifford's paralysis, of the scene where Lady Chatterley cries over the new-born chicks (because she desires a child), of Mellors's occupation as a gamekeeper (symbolic of a force close to the earth), but to the actual descriptions of the union of Lady Chatterley and her lover. Here the rhythm of emotions is associated with the profounder rhythm of nature itself (a feeling familiar to the poets), and Lady Chatterley feels that she is sinking into the deepest sources of creation.

What Lawrence expressed by his intensity of style and feeling is an old philosophic truth, but one concealed from all but the mystics: an experience, provided it is lived with intensity and sincerity, often leads out of itself into its opposite. Novalis called it the "perfection of the absolute" and said: "All absolute sensation is religious."

Many have been shocked by this intensity about sex, but

the truth is that it is just that intensity which led him to describe the "ecstasy of the flesh which transfigures" and to this conception of marriage: "...marriage is no marriage that is not basically and permanently phallic, and that is not linked up with the sun and the earth, the moon and the fixed stars and the planets, in the rhythm of days, in the rhythm of months, in the rhythms of quarters, of years, of decades and of centuries. Marriage is no marriage that is not a correspondence of blood. *For the blood is the substance of the soul,* and of the deepest consciousness."

The realism is thus merely a beginning, a basis.

Our generation has chosen to see in *Lady Chatterley's Lover* only a convenient expression, in strong language, of its revolt from the white idealistic love of the past and a defiant justification of a life of free physical sensation. But if Lawrence had meant to justify mere sensation for its own sake he would have stopped with the descriptions of the physical acts. As it is, one French commentator at least has taken him to task for exalting sexual experience and enveloping it with mysticism.

If, to some, his work is nothing but crude realism, to others who know poetry it is more than that: the prose is lyrical as well as sensual, the descriptions full of sensitiveness as well as crudeness, of beauty as well as obscenity. A vigorous and impetuous style carries the weight of intense physical and imaginative emotions and in the end unites them in a brilliant fusion of physical-mysticism.

Why the crudeness and the obscenity of the language? Because Lawrence was preoccupied with his *beginning,* with making a new beginning in love. And first it was necessary to dethrone mentally directed love. Lawrence never tired of warning us that "the affinity of mind and personality is an excellent basis of friendship between the sexes, but a disastrous basis for marriage." Why? Because it often constitutes a denial of the deeper needs of our nature. So he pleads for an instinctive beginning. He gives us in *Lady Chatterley's Lover* an honest picture of all the aspects and moods of physical love. But he writes neither scientifically nor for the sake of pornography. Even when he is most naturalistic and apparently obscene there is a reason for the obscene words. They are the very words by which Lawrence believed one could alone renew contact with the reality of sexual passion, which the cult of idealism had distorted for us. His war was against evasive, reticent language, which makes for evasive, reticent living and thinking.

Love had been travestied by the idealists. By force of association the words they used aroused lofty exaltations or timorous reactions in the head which had no connection whatever with sensual love and were therefore "counterfeits." Lawrence took the naked words and used them because they conveyed realities which we were to live out not merely in action but in thought. For Lawrence did not mean *Lady Chatterley's Lover* to incite everyone to action in sex; only those who should act must. Modern psychology has told us what becomes of feelings which are not honestly and naturally lived out: they reappear later in perverted forms. It has also told us that no feeling can be awakened in us unless we have the roots of it in ourselves; no ideas can be put into our heads, they can only be developed when the seed of them is already growing in us. *Lady Chatterley's Lover* could do nothing but awaken those who desired to be awakened. For others, the experience has to be gone through, not with the body but with the mind. Lawrence says himself: "This is the real point of the book. I want men and women to be able to *think* sex, fully, completely, honestly and cleanly." Now this cannot be done if we are afraid of words.

When Lawrence had taken Lady Chatterley and Mellors back to the sources and basis of sexual love it was like his imaginative retrogression into the primitive, which, as we have seen, was not a permanent return but only a dipping back, to be refreshed at the source, in order that we might go forward again with renewed strength. In the book, Lady Chatterley and Mellors can go on, because of their fulfillment — she to motherhood, he to the building of their world together, and in the end both to chastity. For now there can be chastity between them. There are few endings as serene as the end of Mellors's letter to Lady Chatterley: "I love the chastity now that it flows between us... We could be chaste together... We really trust in the little flame, and in the unnamed gods that shield it from being blown out... So I believe in the little flame between us. For me it's the only thing in the world..."